Strategy through Personal Values

Scott Lichtenstein · Malcolm Higgs

Strategy through Personal Values

A behavioural approach

palgrave
macmillan

Scott Lichtenstein
Birmingham City Business School
Birmingham, UK

Malcolm Higgs
Southampton Business School
University of Southampton
Southampton, UK

ISBN 978-3-030-88268-6 ISBN 978-3-030-88269-3 (eBook)
https://doi.org/10.1007/978-3-030-88269-3

This Palgrave Macmillan imprint is published by the registered company Springer Nature Switzerland AG
The registered company address is: Gewerbestrasse 11, 6330 Cham, Switzerland

Contents

List of Figures

List of Tables

CHAPTER 1

Why Should Strategy Be Guided by Personal Values?

Abstract This chapter provides a context for a behavioural approach to strategy and the pivotal role of personal values in strategy formulation and implementation. The aim is to provide a brief overview of the topic, highlight its unique contribution to strategy and introduce the strategy-as values-congruence approach. In answering the question of why the strategy should be personal values-guided, the chapter offers an alternative to the rational and deterministic schools of strategy which have been debunked by managers and strategists' cognitive limitations. Moreover, by introducing and discussing personal values-guided strategy, the understanding and practice of strategy can be enhanced. We provide an example to illustrate its relevance and why a personal values-based guidance system matters even more in a volatile, uncertain, complex and ambiguous trading environment.

Keyword Behavioural approach to strategy · Bounded rationality · Cognitive bias · Intellectual and emotional buy-in · Personal values-guided strategy

S. Lichtenstein and M. Higgs, *Strategy through Personal Values*,
https://doi.org/10.1007/978-3-030-88269-3_1

Background

One of the major evolutions in strategy is the insight that particularly in times of disruption the visible outcomes of strategic choices reflect the unconscious forces guiding those judgements, chief among them being our personal values. As one team of research psychologists observed, '*Indeed, it seems fair to say that whenever the phenomenon of interest involves choice, or preferences, values are likely to be a crucial, explanatory construct*' (Mumford et al., 2002, p. 348).

In a rarefied academic environment, educators may get away with presenting students with 'widget factories', rivals' costs, and the demand curve based on a premise of strategy as a deterministic rational calculus, but in the work world that is far more complex with office politics and real people the linkage between actions and outcomes are far from clear. Strategy as a calculative rationality in an organisational context is an abstraction.

1.1 Rationality Isn't Rational: Cognitive Bias in Strategy

One of the fastest-growing areas in management that has gone mainstream has been behavioural economics and strategy, which has exposed the limits of rationality. Concepts such as 'the planning fallacy', 'over optimism', 'attribution error', 'anchoring' and 'competitor neglect' are just some of the cognitive biases that managers and leadership suffer from. Indeed, these have entered our common lexicon. Cognitive biases are referred to as blind spots that reduce thinking accuracy and result in inaccurate—and often irrational—conclusions (Heick, 2019).

In investing, three cognitive biases are well known to affect decisions (Index Fund Advisors, 2018), the first of which also relates to strategy and 'big shopping' like mergers and acquisitions:

- Over-confidence bias—thinking returns will be bigger than they are likely to achieve,
- Hindsight bias—thinking past events were predictable when they weren't, and
- Regret avoidance—never to repeat the same decision if it resulted in a significant loss or a big gain.

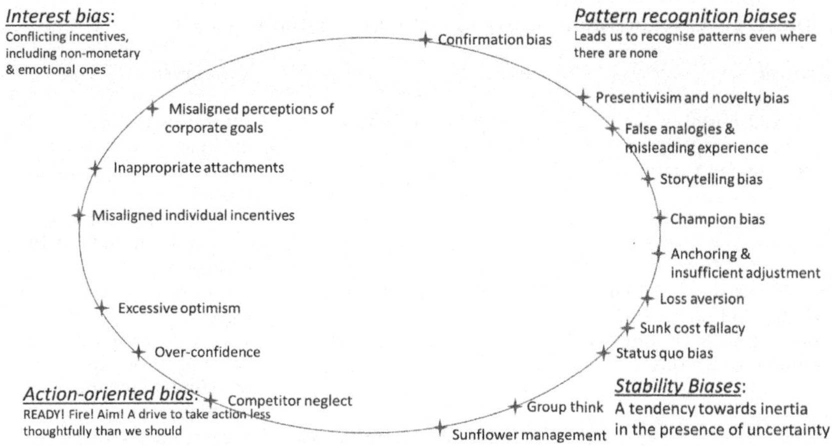

Fig. 1.1 Strategy-oriented cognitive biases (*Source* Adapted from Lovallo and Sibony [2010])

Below (see Fig. 1.1), the main strategy-oriented failures of rational and critical thinking from Lovallo and Sibony (2010) are mapped onto four main categorisations of cognitive biases: (i) Pattern recognition bias; (ii) Stability bias; (iii) Action-oriented bias; and (iv) Interest bias:

In Table 1.1, we further categorise the biases and their definitions into the heuristics that underpin them.

From all these biases, the most important bias from our perspective is *confirmation bias*, defined as 'the seeking or interpreting of evidence in ways that are partial to existing beliefs', which accounts for a significant element of disputes among individuals, groups and nations (Nickerson, 1988, p. 175). Have you had the 'conviction trap' experience of your partner who asks you to go to the cupboard and get a spice, say oregano? You look and look and then exclaim, 'I can't see it'. Convinced it's there, s/he asks you to look harder which you do until again you exclaim 'I can't see it, it's not here'. At this point s/he comes over and grabs it right from in front of your face! Our convictions can literally blind us.

Table 1.1 Categorisation of strategy-oriented cognitive biases

Concept	*Biases*	*Description*
To avoid mistakes, we're motivated to preserve our autonomy and status in a group	Misaligned individual incentives	Incentives for individuals in organisations to adopt views or to seek outcomes favourable to their unit or themselves, at the expense of overall interests of the company
We favour simple-looking options and complete information over complex, ambiguous options	Inappropriate attachments	Emotional attachment of individuals to people or elements of the business (such as legacy products or brands) creating a misalignment of interests
	Misaligned perceptions of corporate goals	Disagreements (often unspoken) about the hierarchy or relative weight of objectives pursued by the organisation and about the trade-offs between them
To get things done, we tend to complete things we've invested time & money in	Excessive optimism	The tendency for people to be overoptimistic about the outcome of planned actions, to overestimate the likelihood of negative ones
To act, we must be confident we can make an impact and feel what we do is important	Overconfidence	Overestimating our skill level relative to others', leading us to overestimate our ability to affect future outcomes, take credit for past outcomes, and neglect the role of chance
To stay focuses, we favour the immediate, relatable thing in front of us	Competitor neglect	The tendency to plan without factoring in competitive responses, as if one's playing tennis against a wall, not a live opponent
We are drawn to details that confirm our existing beliefs	Confirmation bias	The overweighting of evidence consistent with a favoured belief, underweighting evidence against a favoured belief, or failure to search impartially for evidence

(continued)

Table 1.1 (continued)

Concept	*Biases*	*Description*
Bizarre/funny//visually striking/ anthropomorphic things stick out more than the non-bizarre/unfunny things	Presentivisim and novelty bias	Generalising based on examples that are particularly recent or memorable
We fill in characteristics from stereotypes, generalities, and prior histories	False analogies—especially, misleading experiences	Relying on comparisons with situations that are not directly comparable
We find stories and patterns even in sparse data	Power of storytelling	The tendency to remember and to believe more easily a set of facts when they are presented in a story
We notice things already primed in memory or repeated often	Anchoring and insufficient adjustment	Rooting oneself to an initial value, leading to insufficient adjustments of subsequent estimates
We simplify probabilities and numbers to make them easier to think about	Loss aversion	The tendency to feel losses more acutely than gains of the same amount, making us more risk averse than a rational calculation would suggest
We project our current mindset and assumptions onto the past and future	Sunk-cost fallacy	Paying attention to historical costs that are non-recoverable when considering future courses of action
We imagine things and people we are familiar with or fond of or better than us	Champion bias	The tendency to evaluate a plan or proposal based on the track record of the person presenting it, more than on the facts supporting it
	Status quo bias	Preference for the status quo in the absence of pressure to change it
	Groupthink	Striving for consensus at the cost of a realistic appraisal of alternative courses of action
	Sunflower management	Tendency for groups to align with the views of their leaders, whether expressed or assumed

Source Adapted from Lovallo and Sibony (2010) and Heik (2019)

1.2 Strategy as Values Congruence

The significance of confirmation bias in strategy is that we all evaluate information and strategies in line with our convictions, values and attitudes and skew information in a way that supports what we already value and believe to be true (Mosckowitz, 2005; Robinson, 2015). Therefore, strategy is value-laden: if a strategy de-values what someone has a conviction about they will ignore, evade or at worst, sabotage it. To get true buy-in requires intellectual and emotional buy-in such that those who implement it understand what the strategy and desired ends are, and are willing and committed to execute, respectively.

To executive strategy firstly requires intellectual buy-in such that people grasp it, and even that threshold is not being met in many firms according to some estimates that have found 95% of employees don't know or understand what their company strategy is (Hunter & O'Shannasy, 2007; Kaplan & Norton, 2005). More importantly, however, is emotional buy-in at the level of personal values. Willingness to implement strategy only happens when strategy fits what one values (Updhyay et al., 2013). A strategy without a commitment at the level of personal values-based is a delusion. Hence, this pivot promotes the *strategy-as-values-congruence* perspective: strategic leaders' primary concern should be with identifying their personal values and translating the organisation's purpose, goals and strategies into the operative personal values of direct reports and employees for intellectual and emotional buy-in to execute strategy. What strategy gets personal values-guided commitment gets done.

1.3 A Behavioural Approach

Insight into the behavioural factors influencing strategy is by no means recent, although some have been slow to 'get the memo'. Its roots lie in Cyert and March's (1963) *A behavioral theory of the firm*, which at its crux is the notion that managers were only 'boundedly rational', i.e. they never had perfect information, were pressed for time and didn't devise optimal solutions; instead, they choose between competing demands. At the base of the behavioural approach is the startling assumption that in order to understand strategy, one must understand strategists (Hambrick, 2007) including ourselves.

Even the most ardent proponents of the rational, deterministic school of strategy such as Michael Porter (2008) identified the personal values of those formulating and implement strategy as one of the four pillars of strategy, as shown in Fig. 1.2, even if he never pursued it. One way to read Fig. 1.2 is to note that strategy is a combination of rational inputs at the top corners and behavioural factors of strategy on the bottom corners.

Our emotions and strategic decisions are guided by our personal values whether we are aware of it or not, an example of which is provided at the end of this chapter. Definitions of personal values can be found throughout literature in psychology and business, but common amongst them is the idea that personal values are emotional states concerning what individuals think is important in life, that when threatened disturbs us at an unconscious level (e.g. Schwartz, 2012). They are motivational domains that guide one's thoughts and actions as desirable goals people strive to attain (e.g. England, 1967; Guth and Tagiuri, 1965; Rokeach, 1979). Personal values are an unconscious power for understanding interpersonal and organisational life (Posner & Schmidt, 1994).

The relationship between the personal values of executives and strategic decisions has been the subject of much debate (e.g. Hambrick, 2007). Executives' personal values in companies large and small are believed

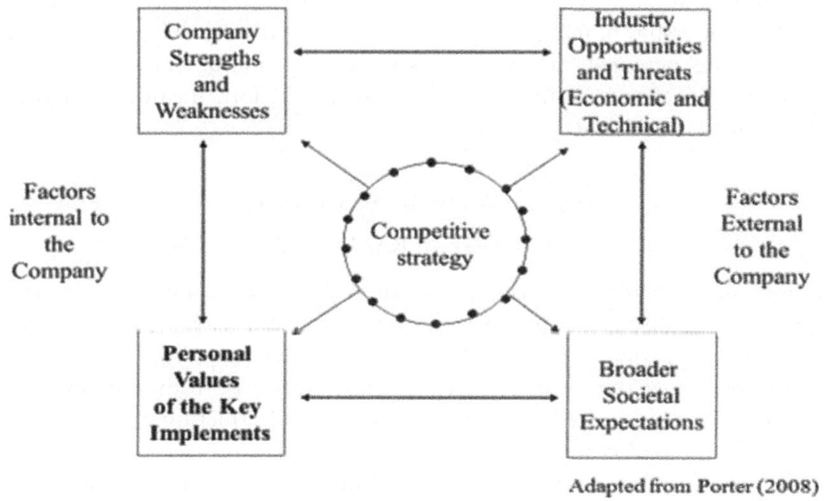

Fig. 1.2 Key determinants of strategy

to impact upon strategic choice and performance directly and indirectly (Finkelstein et al., 2009). Decisions determining the most sensible economic strategy for a company are proposed as being intimately linked with the personal values of those who make the choice (Andrews, 1987; Porter, 2008). The personal values of top managers are reflected in the aims of an enterprise and have the profoundest impact on the direction in which a firm moves and the way it operates (Andrews, 1987; Hambrick & Brandon, 1988; Steiner, 1969).

In truth, this chapter's question shouldn't be '*Why should strategy be guided by personal values?*', it is '*In what ways is strategy guided by our personal values?*', which is the subject of next chapter. This latter question invites a certain responsibility of strategists.

1.3.1 Strategy Is Personal

Where do strategies come from? Our minds: imagination, ingenuity and inventiveness, through social interaction. Healthy minds create healthy strategies, unhealthy minds create unhealthy strategies. What separates Strategy from other fields such as Marketing or Economics is that whilst these fields expose the biases in *others*, strategic leaders are required to uncover the biases and personal values in *themselves* as well as others (Lovallo & Sibony, 2010). Therefore, it behoves strategists to learn and use the leadership practice of *personal values sensitivity*, defined as tuning into all the personal values, interests, beliefs and motivational drivers present in important communication and interaction, starting with your own (McKenzie & Aitken, 2012).

1.4 Why Is Personal Values-Guided Strategy Relevant?

From a management perspective, we are in the midst of a publicly-quoted company viability crisis that existed even before the Corona virus, which is likely to get more acute with the disruptions to come. Figure 1.3 clearly indicates the consequences of short-term, bottom-line thinking that is endemic in chasing quarterly targets and afflicting the longevity of publicly traded companies.

If human longevity were in such decline they would call it a public health crisis. Why is this not considered a management crisis? It's estimated that 82 million employees in 195 countries work for publicly

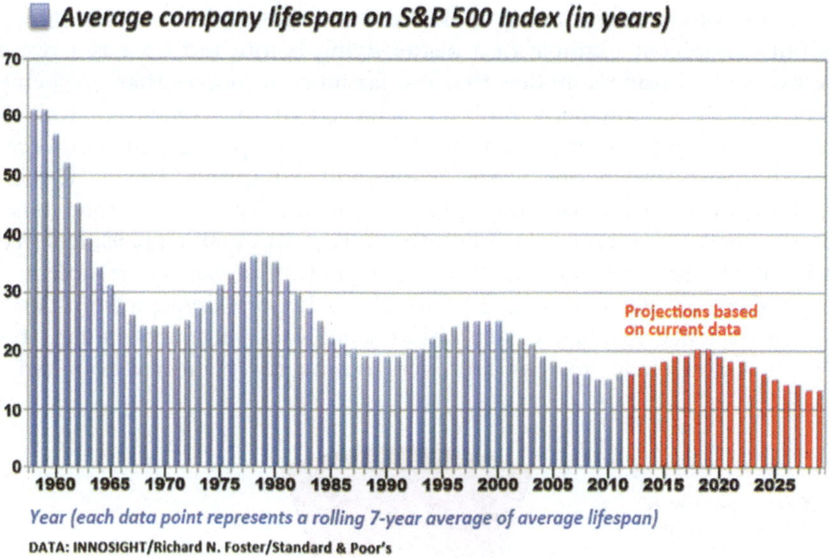

Fig. 1.3 Declining shareholder company lifespan

traded companies worldwide (Index Fund Advisors, 2018) making its impact noteworthy. And yet, despite the fact that only 10% of the world's economically active population work for publicly owned shareholding limited companies quoted on stock exchanges, the discourse around business is dominated by the shareholder capital model through everyday business media projection that profit maximisation, and the concomitant accountability to an elite group of shareholders/owners, is the only game in town (Pless et al., 2012). This narrative is increasingly devoid of concern for a well-functioning community within its natural ecosystem. Citizens, strategists and economists are increasingly calling for a more sophisticated conceptualisation of capitalism and industrialisation, imbued with reciprocity and shared reward (Porter & Cramer, 2011). Incrementalism, reformist and transformational strategies that align with people's personal values are discussed in more depth in Chapter 5 to mobilise the emotional, material and intellectual resources required to allow organisations and internal and external stakeholders to prepare, adapt and navigate the challenges and continued disruptions the business landscape faces.

Scores of Canadians being cooked from the inside from a 'heat dome' is but one recent example of a planet dying before our eyes as a result of extractive business models that use far more resources than are being replenished. Sustainability can't be achieved in the context of today's humanity using the equivalent of 1.6 Earths to provide the resources we use and absorb our waste (Ecological Footprint, 2021). Rather, more wholistic personal values-guided regenerative strategies and business models are emerging based on the realisation by strategic leaders that a company can't be 'sustainable' if it degrades the very environment it depends upon. Raworth's (2020) Doughnut Report, drawing from Earth systems science (Steffen et al., 2015) graphically illustrates in Fig. 1.4 on the outer circle how we are overshooting the planetary boundaries

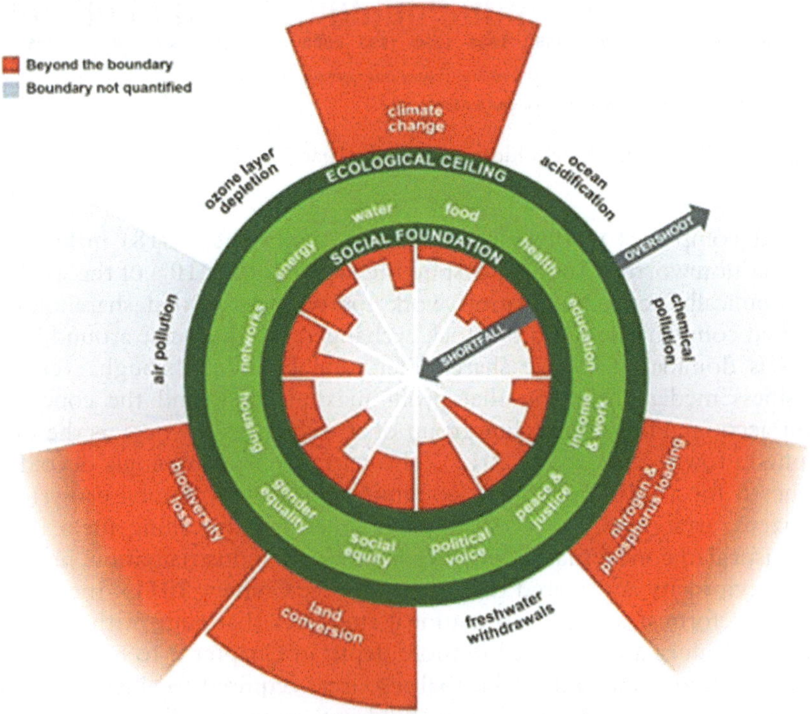

Fig. 1.4 Doughnut Transgression (*Source* Doughnut Report [2020])

of climate change, ocean acidification, chemical pollution, nitrogen & phosphorus loading, freshwater withdrawals, land conversion, biodiversity loss, air pollution and ozone layer depletion, whilst on the inner circle undershooting human needs as defined by the United Nation's Sustainability Development Goals agreed by 193 member countries in 2015 to be achieved by 2030 (UN, 2015).

1.4.1 The Need for Strategists' Inner Compass in a Volatility, Uncertainty, Complexity and Ambiguity (VUCA) World

Personal values guide the choices we make, the people we trust, the appeals we respond to, and the way we invest our time and energy (Posner & Schmidt, 1994). In turbulent times, personal values give a sense of direction amid conflicting views and demands. Uncovering the invisible forces guiding our thoughts and emotions is ever more important in a time where our world is experiencing ever more massive disruptions to our normal pattern of behaviour including AI & robotics and a variety of inter-related Geopolitical, Economic, Social, Technological and Environmental factors, as seen in Fig. 1.5.

1.5 Mini Case: Sully's Inner Compass that Saved 155 Lives

Just how personal values gives a sense of direction amid conflicting views and demands is illustrated by the personal values-guided strategic choices made by Captain Chesley 'Sully' Sullenberger on US Airways Flight 1549 In January 2009.

Most of us won't ever have to steer an Airbus A320 full of passengers onto the Hudson River moments after suffering a 'VUCA' event of a flock of birds knocking out both engines, but Chesley 'Sully' Sullenberger and Jeffrey Skiles did. In January 2009, they safely landed US Airways Flight 1549 in the Hudson River off Midtown Manhattan, and remarkably, all 155 passengers and crew survived with only minor injuries.

> I was telling my older daughter what integrity meant to me and I said it was about doing the right thing even if it's not convenient. I might tell her now it's having **real values** and choosing to live by them. Captain Sullenberg said. (Waiki, 2011, p. 1)

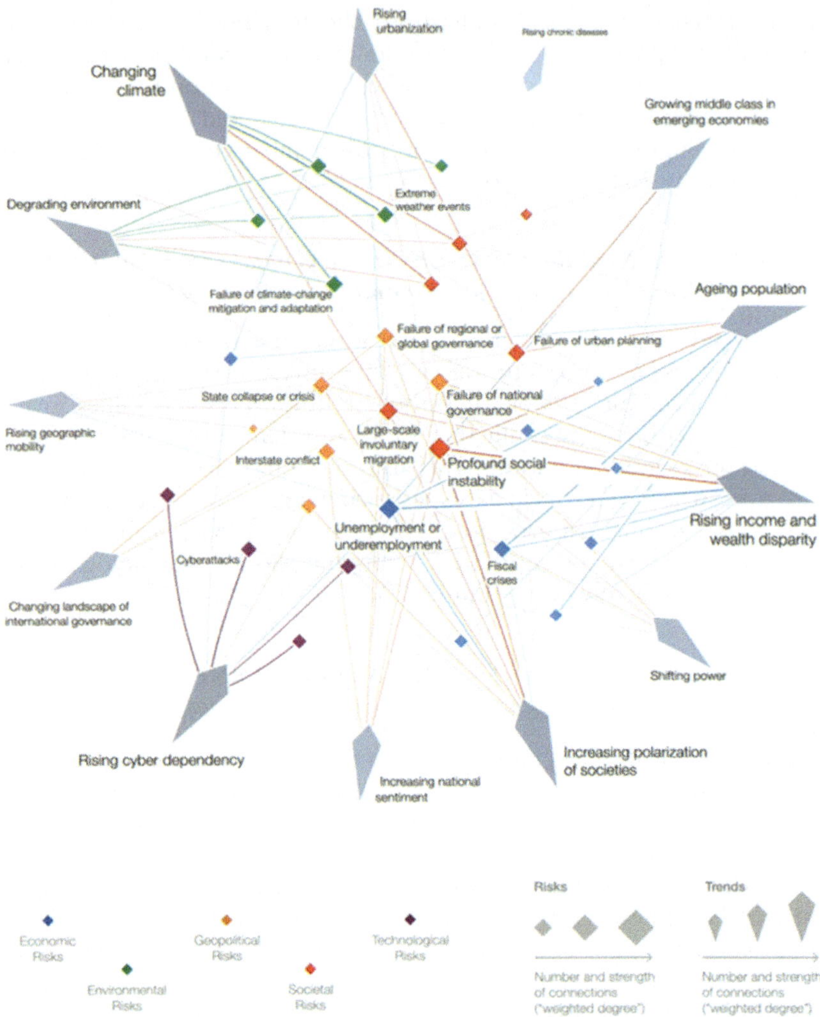

Fig. 1.5 Global risk perception survey (*Source* World Economic Forum)

He also said strategic leadership is about sacrificing short-term gain for the long-term, however personally awkward. If you know the full story, you'll know how personally awkward this event became for him: although he was considered a hero, the National Transportation Safety Board indicted him for 'pilot error' for neither returning to LaGuardia nor landing at another airport, Teterboro airport. An inditement would have resulted in him losing his pilot licence. He was later to recount that he had flown thousands of flights in the last 42 years, "*But now*," he says, "*my entire career is being judged by how I performed on one of them*" (Zaslow, 2009, p. 1).

Sully sites his upbringing, family bonds and his own crucibles of experience for his sense of integrity in Sullenberger's (2009) book *Highest Duty: My Search for What Really Matters*. In US Navy aviation training, Sullenberger investigated the air-crew ejection study where he learned that many pilots waited too long before ejecting from planes that were about to crash. Why? Many feared retribution if they lost a million-dollar jet: they were determined to try to save their airplanes, putting profit before their own lives.

"As soon as the birds struck," he says, "I could have tried to return to LaGuardia so as not to ruin a US Airways aircraft. I could have worried that my decision to ditch the plane would be questioned by superiors or investigators. But I chose not to. By attempting a water landing, I would sacrifice the 'airplane goal'—trying not to destroy an aircraft valued at $60 million—for the goal of saving lives" (Zaslow, 2009). His personal values gave him a sense of direction: his inner compass valued people over profit, which prepared him for that moment, which resulted in a choice and action that saved the lives of everyone on board.[1]

Questions

Am I aware of how my inner compass, the convictions and personal values that guide my decisions?

Is this reflected in my personal or organisational strategy? How the links between my inner compass and strategy be more explicit? Is my team and I role modelling it?

[1] Spoiler alert: the computer simulations simulated diversions to LaGuardia and to Teterboro airport with both resulting in crashes.

1.5.1 Top Management's Inner Compass

In a prescient article in The Economist at the turn of this century, Peter Drucker (2001), the Austrian pracademic claimed an important task for top management in the next society's corporation will be to balance its three dimensions: as an *economic*, *human* and as an increasingly important *social* organisation. The biggest challenge will be its *social legitimacy*: it's values, mission and vision. Increasingly, he argued, top management will represent the unique personality of the company. Drucker couldn't have foreseen the pandemic, but COVID-19 has put companies 'inner compass' in the spotlight. The social media reaction to Chief Financial Officer Chris Wootton and CEO Mike Ashley's public letter to Boris Johnson insisting that Sports Direct should stay open after the 'lockdown' announcement because selling fitness equipment makes it an 'essential business' was met with contempt and anger. Even after it agreed to close, reports emerged of staff being instructed to go to work as normal, as were thousands of others on zero-hours contracts (Sutton, 2020). Similarly, the UK pub chain JD Wetherspoon has been accused of abandoning its 43,000 staff, saying it cannot afford to pay them until it is reimbursed by the government's 'furlough' scheme, which pays 80% of employees' wages. Chairman Tim Martin instead advised staff to seek work in Tesco. The hashtag #boycottWetherspoon trended on Twitter. A picture was circulating of the Wetherspoon's pub in Crystal Palace, with the slogan 'Pay your staff' daubed in paint across the windows.

Contrast this with UK retailer Pret a Manger, which was one of the first to offer free hot drinks and half-price food for NHS staff prior to having to close, or Dominos offering free pizza to NHS staff. Zipcar was providing free car journeys for NHS staff to get to and from work, while BrewDog has started manufacturing hand sanitiser to provide for free to hospitals in need (Sutton, 2020).

These examples illustrate that *altruism* and *empathy* are currency of social legitimacy in a VUCA world, and a judging society will continue to scrutinise the inner compasses of top management.

1.6 Summary

In this chapter, why should strategy be explicitly guided by personal values has been addressed. Whilst strategy has traditionally been considered rational and deterministic, behavioural economists and strategists have more recently been examining strategy at work which provides new insights into cognitive traps and the influence of the unconscious power of personal values in guiding strategy. The relevance of personal values guided strategy was discussed in the context of shortening publicly-traded lifespans and the Anthropocene challenges of planetary boundaries which exposes the failure of short-term, bottom-line thinking and the need for wholistic strategies that are reflective of people's deep reservoir of emotional resource. In a VUCA world and business climate where businesses have to work ever harder to gain social legitimacy, a values-guided compass for strategic decisions gives direction amidst conflicting demands and is increasingly important sought by internal and external stakeholders.

Bibliography

Andrews, K. (1987). *The concept of corporate strategy*. Dow Jones-Irwin Inc.

Cyert, R. M., & March, J. G. (1963). A behavioral theory of the firm. *Englewood Cliffs, NJ, 2*(4), 169–187.

Drucker, P. (2001, November 3). The next society. *The Economist*. Special issue.

Ecological Footprint. (2021). https://www.footprintnetwork.org/our-work/ecological-footprint/. Accessed 13 July 2021.

England, G. W. (1967). Personal value systems of American managers. *Academy of Management Journal, 10*(1), 53–68.

Finkelstein, S., Hambrick, D. C., & Cannella, A. A. (2009). *Strategic leadership: Theory and research on executives, top management teams, and boards*. Oxford University Press.

Guth, W. D., & Taguri, R. (1965). Personal values and corporate strategy. *Harvard Business Review, 43*(5), 123–132.

Hambrick, D. C. (2007). Upper echelons theory: An update. *Academy of Management Review, 32*(2), 334–343.

Hambrick, D. C., & Brandon, G. L. (1988). Executive values. In D. C. Hambrick (Ed.), *The executive effect: Concepts and methods for studying top managers* (pp. 3–34). JAI Press.

Heick, T. (2019, October 14). *The Cognitive Bias Codex: A Visual Of 180+ Cognitive Biases*. Critical Thinking. https://www.teachthought.com/critical-thinking/the-cognitive-bias-codex-a-visual-of-180-cognitive-biases/. Accessed 23 March 2020.

Hunter, P., & O'Shannasy, T. (2007). Contemporary strategic management in Australia: 'Back to the future in the 2000s.' *Singapore Management Review, 29*(2), 21–36.

Index Fund Advisors. (2018). *Index Funds: The Movie*.

Innosight. (2020). *Corporate Longevity*. https://www.ecosia.org/images?q=corporate+longeavity+innosight#id=65B2FBA3CA15C0DF5161C3C12C5826FB7CBEF629. Accessed 29 March 2020.

Kaplan, R. S., & Norton, D. P. (2005). *Creating the office of strategy management*. Division of Research, Harvard Business School.

Lovallo, D., & Sibony, O. (2010). The case for behavioral strategy. *McKinsey Quarterly, 2*(1), 30–43.

McKenzie, J., & Aitken, P. (2012). Learning to lead the knowledgeable organization: Developing leadership agility. *Strategic HR Review, 11*(6), 329–334.

Moskowitz, G. B. (2005/2013). *Social cognition: Understanding self and others*. The Guilford Press.

Mumford, M. D., Connelly, M. S., Helton, W. B.,Van Doorn, J. R., & Osburn, H. K. (2002). Alternative approaches for measuring values: Direct and indirect assessments for performance prediction. *Journal of Vocational Behavior, 61*(2), 348–373.

Nickerson, R. S. (1988). Confirmation bias: A Ubiquitous phenomenon in many guises. *Review of General Psychology, 2*(2), 175–220.

Pless, N. M., Maak, T., & Waldman, D. A. (2012). Different approaches toward doing the right thing: Mapping the responsibility orientations of leaders. *Academy of Management Perspectives, 26*(4), 51–65.

Porter, M. E. (2008). *Competitive strategy: Techniques for analyzing industries and competitors*. Simon and Schuster.

Porter, M. E., & Cramer, M. R. (2011, January–February). Creating shared value. *Harvard Business Review*, pp. 62–77.

Posner, B. Z., & Schmidt, W. H. (1994). An updated look at the values and expectations of federal government executives. *Public Administration Review, 54*, 20–24.

Powell, T. C., Lovallo, D., & Fox, C. R. (2011). Behavioral strategy. *Strategic Management Journal, 32*(13), 1369–1386.

Raworth, K. (2020). *Doughnut Report*. https://commons.wikimedia.org/wiki/File:Doughnut-transgressing.jpg. Accessed 13 July 2021.

Robinson, E. (2015). *The psychology of change in organisations: Mindsets and the paradox of continuity* (Doctoral dissertation). University of Cambridge.

Rokeach, M. (1979). From individual to institutional values with special reference to the values of science. In M. Rokeach (Ed.), *Understanding human values* (pp. 47–70). Free Press.

Schwartz, S. H. (2012). An overview of the Schwartz theory of basic values. *Online Readings in Psychology and Culture, 2*(1), 2307–2919.

Steffen, W., Richardson, K., Rockström, J., Cornell, S. E., Fetzer, I., Bennett, E. M., Biggs, R., Carpenter, Stephen R., Vries, W. de, Wit, C. A. de, Folke, C., Gerten, D., Heinke, J., Mace, G. M., Persson, L. M., Ramanathan, V., Reyers,

B., & Sorlin, S. (2015). Planetary boundaries: Guiding human development on a changing planet. *Science, 347*(6223).
Steiner, G. (1969). *Top management planning*. Macmillan.
Sullenberger, C. (2009). *Highest duty: My search for what really matters*. William Morrow/HarperCollins Publishers.
Sutton, P. (2020, March 26). *We won't forget the businesses that treat their Staff—And us—Badly*. HuffingtonPost.
United nations. (2015). *Sustainable Development Goals*. https://sdgs.un.org/goals. Accessed 13 July 2021.
Upadhyay, A. Y. A., Upadhyay, A. K., & Palo, S. (2013). Strategy implementation using balanced scorecard: Achieving success through personal values of leaders and employees. *Management and Labour Studies, 38*(4), 447–469.
Waki, N. (2011, January 26). *Hudson pilot tells business leaders to look beyond short-term*. Davos Notebook.
World Economic Forum. (2020). *Global Risk Perception Survey*. https://www.ecosia.org/images?q=world+economic+forum+global+risk+perception+202#id=E499913F07846E7DC3151BE26B4A93EF7A2C90DB. Accessed 29 March 2020.
Zaslow, J. (2009, October 14). *What we can learn from Sully's Journey*. WSJ.

CHAPTER 2

Personal Values and Strategic Choice

Abstract Our suggested contributions to this chapter are fourfold. Firstly, we introduce a model to help explore the link between personal values and strategic choice. Secondly, we summarise research results concerning the significant role personal values play in guiding strategic decisions in the workplace. Next, we introduce a framework to understand how manager's values orientations manifest in predictable patterns of strategic choices. Finally, the application of values orientation to strategic decisions in the context, the values dynamic of an organisation is illustrated through two mini case studies with questions for managers and leaders to reflect upon to draw implications for their own strategic leadership.

Keywords Strategic choice · Upper echelon theory · Congruency theory · Leadership-strategy match · Personal Values orientation

Kurt Lewin (1951) once said, "There's nothing so practical as good theory"—because good theory guides effective action by turning knowledge into wisdom. Hence, in this section, the three main theoretical underpinnings of the personal values strategic and choice relationship are reviewed to aid in its understanding for application.

S. Lichtenstein and M. Higgs, *Strategy through Personal Values*,
https://doi.org/10.1007/978-3-030-88269-3_2

2.1 Personal Values-Strategy Theory

The Upper echelon theory, Congruency theory and the leadership-strategy match are introduced with relevant empirical findings, which provides a conceptual foundation to the relationship between manager-leaders' values and strategic choice.

2.1.1 *The Upper Echelon Theory*

The most important conceptual development linking personal values to strategic choice and performance is Hambrick and Mason's (1984) upper echelon theory, that has over 13,000 citations, which was later built upon by Finkelstein and Hambrick (1996). The upper echelon theory made the crucial link between managers' values, cognitive base, selective perception and strategic choice as seen in Fig. 2.1.

The conceptual model of the research in Fig. 2.1 illustrates how personal values filter strategic leaders' perceptions of the situations about which they make strategic choices. Ismail (2016, p. 29) explains the process of how personal values shape strategic choice which is illustrated in the conceptual model as phases 1–3: (1) field of vision (the directions they look and listen), (2) selective perception (what they actually see and hear), and (3) and interpretation (how they attach meaning to what they see and hear).

Hambrick and Mason's (1984) theory built upon previous work such as Postman et al. (1948, p. 143) who demonstrated that "personal values are demonstrable determinants of what the individual selects perceptually from his environment". This model has formed the basis for establishing

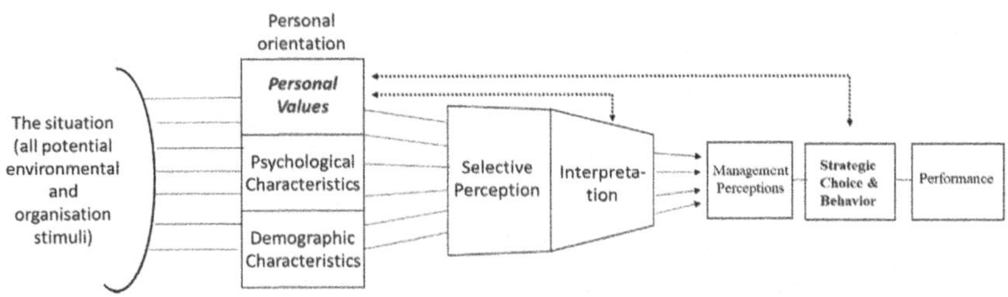

Fig. 2.1 The upper echelon theory (*Source* Adapted from Hambrick and Mason [1984], Finkelstein and Hambrick [1996])

that strategic leadership orientation is influenced by psychological characteristics, cognitive biases (Finkelstein & Hambrick, 1996), personality (Schyns & Felfe, 2006), and demographic characteristics such as the age, sex and social class of an individual (Thomas & Ramaswamy, 1996). Lichtenstein's (2005) research based on 167 managers found that executives' personal values had a significant impact on performance and a greater impact on performance than demographic variables, the latter supporting the notion that personal values are more crucial in the casual chain of fundamental characteristics of executives than age, gender or education.

As discussed in the last chapter, the upper echelon theory is based on the alternative to the 'rational wo/men' assumption and instead assumes 'bounded rationality', i.e. that managers don't have unlimited time and information, the optimum strategy is unknowable and managers' rationality is bounded by their personal values that are 'perceptual screens' that filter out information and focuses priorities (England, 1967; Hambrick & Brandon, 1988). If you've ever experienced the phenomenon of buying a red sweater and all of a sudden you begin seeing people wearing red sweaters everywhere or have just broken up with a boy/girlfriend and then every song you hear is either the blues or about a broken heart, you'll understand the effect personal values has in focusing attention (and intention).

This model underscores Hambrick and Brandon's (1988) work that asserts that personal values act in two ways: (i) indirectly in terms of perceptual screening and (ii) directly in terms of channelling behaviour, i.e. that managers choose strategies that are congruent with their personal values.

Personal values theorists England and Lee (1974) identified at least seven ways in which a manager's often unconscious personal values have an impact upon sense-making and sense-giving. Personal values:

(i) Influence managers' perceptions of situations,
(ii) Affect the solutions they generate,
(iii) Impact the quantity and quality of interpersonal relationships,
(iv) Influence perceptions of individual and organisational success,
(v) Provide a basis for determining ethical behaviour,
(vi) Affect the extent to which managers accept or reject particular organisational pressures and goals, and
(vii) Focus and shape managerial performance.

The Upper Echelon Theory is silent about whether the personal values that guide senior management has to be reasonable or ethical, which could be construed as a shortcoming of the theory. Moreover, whilst senior managers' personal values function in the same way as do employees', suppliers', owners' and other stakeholders' values, one could argue that the model oversimplifies what is in fact a dynamic of multiple stakeholders' values (Freeman et al., 1988). We address these shortcomings in Chapter 5 discussion of moral orientations and how they apply to multiple stakeholders. Finally, the theory does not discuss the inter-relationships between senior managers' personal values and other organisation factors, which Congruency theory outlined below does address.

2.1.2 Congruency Theory

The underlying premise of Congruency theory proposed by Nightingale and Toulouse (1977) is that in an organisational environment, personal values, structure, process and reaction or adjustment strategies are inter-correlated and must be in congruence for the organisation to be effective. They further explain that the value system of people in positions of authority and responsibility influences the structure and strategy of the organisation. In other words, key organisational leaders structure firms and devise strategic plans in ways that are consistent with their personal values.

Despite the importance of personal values in Nightingale and Toulouse's (1977) congruence model, most research to establish the validity of congruency theory has chosen to focus on CEO personality variables (e.g., locus of control), rather than on their personal values (Ling et al., 2007; Miller et al., 1982). This underscores the early-stage nature of personal values-based strategy research, in part because it's difficult to get access to senior leaders willing to have their personal values probed, and until relatively recently valid and reliable methods to uncover personal values didn't exist and/or were not known to strategy researchers.

A notable exception to the void in the personal values component in congruency research is Ling et al.'s (2007) study of 92 small-to-medium-sized enterprises examining the links between founder–CEOs' personal values (*Collectivism and Novelty*) and their new ventures' performance. Using congruence theory, they hypothesised that founder–CEOs' values concerning *Collectivism*—the subordination of personal interests to the goals of the larger workgroup, an emphasis on sharing, cooperation and group harmony, a concern with group welfare, and hostility towards out-group members (Morris & Davis, 1994, p. 598)—exerted stronger beneficial effects in older and larger firms, whereas personal values concerning *Novelty*—an individuals' tendency to value change, the new, and the different (Hambrick & Brandon, 1988)—exerted stronger beneficial effects in younger firms.[1] They demonstrated that the relationship between founder–CEOs' values of *Novelty* and firm performance was significantly different in young firms[2] and founder–CEOs' values of *Collectivism* were positively related to firm performance amongst older firms.[3]

Whilst this is a welcomed addition to the research evidence into personal values impact upon leaders' influence on organisations, a limitation of the study is that it focuses on a single value—*Novelty* or *Collectivism*, which has been criticised for not considering potentially other important values. Nevertheless, it's a step in the right direction which is crying out for further research.

Having briefly reviewed congruency theory and empirical evidence, the next section covers the final conceptual foundation to the personal values-strategy link, the leadership-strategy match.

2.1.3 Leadership-Strategy Match

The leadership-strategy match perspective is perhaps less a theory than a proposition that there is no strategic leader for all seasons (Rothschild, 1993), and strategic leaders' attributes including personal values need to be aligned or 'fit' the strategy challenge, otherwise, disaster is likely to result. If we just put our common-sense hat on for a moment, it seems obvious that a control freak in charge of R&D or a 'Blue sky' type person in charge of logistics is a car crash ready to happen.

Rothschild's (1993) typology shown in Fig. 2.2 posited the leadership-strategy match approach indicating that different types of strategic leaders

[1] Collectivism and Novelty are not based on Schwartz's values system. Novelty is a sub-dimension of Stimulation but there is no equivalent to Collectivism in Schwartz's values inventory.

[2] ($p < .01$).

[3] ($p < .01$).

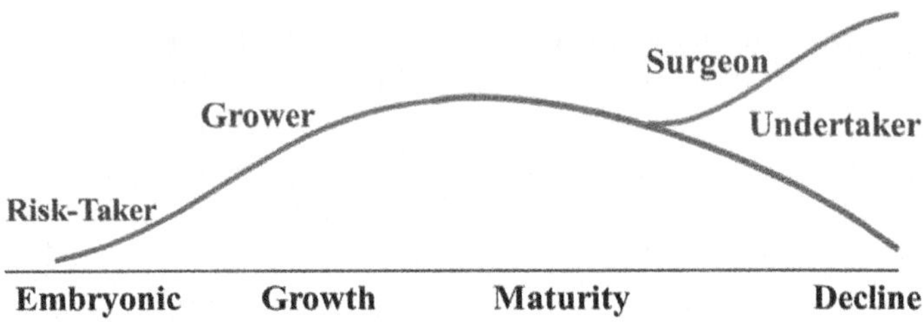

Fig. 2.2 Strategic leadership styles (*Source* Adapted from Rothschild [1993])

are needed at different stages of an organisation's lifecycle, similar to Ling et al.'s (2007) research covered in the previous section.

The leadership-strategy perspective is underpinned by the following propositions:

i. Effective implementation of a strategy depends on a match between individual personality including personal values and the job (Gupta & Govindarajan, 1984).
ii. Managers whose skills, management styles and behaviours are congruent with particular strategies will perform better than those that do not (Hambrick & Mason, 1984; Rothschild, 1993; Szilagyi & Schweiger, 1984), and
iii. Coalignment between managerial characteristics and strategy is necessary to ensure a match between the distinctive competencies of the organisation and management decisions (Thomas et al., 1991).

Thomas and Ramaswamy's (1996) study of 269 managers in Fortune 500 companies is a significant study in the leadership-strategy match approach. They examined the performance impact of manager-strategy coalignment. They found that organisations pursuing distinctly dissimilar strategies—Defenders who defend their product/market position and Prospectors who prospect new products/markets—were led by managers possessing distinctly dissimilar attributes. Moreover, they also found that the strategy-manager match had a positive impact on performance, and a greater explanatory power of performance than either firm size, age or industry membership (Thomas & Ramaswamy, 1996).

Although these are important findings, their research suffers from being based on secondary data and using demographic variables as proxies for underlying psychological attributes. In their study ***innovativeness*** and ***risk-taking*** were measured by age; younger managers are associated with these characteristics, whilst older managers were associated with risk-aversion and being conservative. Similarly, the number of years of formal education was used as a measure of ***open-mindedness*** and ***creativity***.

The use of demographic variables as surrogate measures of managerial characteristics has been severely criticised (e.g. Galavan et al., 2003; Lawrence, 1997; Pettigrew, 1992; Pfeffer, 1983), prompting Hambrick (2007, p. 334) to assert, "... that the use of demographic indicators leaves us at a loss as to the real psychological and social processes that are driving executive behaviour, which is the well-known 'black box problem' (Lawrence, 1997)." Finkelstein and Hambrick (1996, p. 107) beseech future researchers to avoid the use of demographic variables such as age and tenure and instead "to go one step back in the causal chain and use data on the fundamental characteristics of executives themselves (such as their risk orientation, cognitive style, **values**, tenure in their company, functional background)".

With this caveat in mind, Thomas and Ramaswamy's (1996), like Ling et al.'s (2007), research does provide evidence for the personal values strategic choice link. We return in this chapter to further research into the link between personal values and strategic decisions, choices and preferences but to give it meaning we firstly cover the content of personal values in the next section to explore how decisions, choices and preferences vary by different personal values orientations.

2.2 Making Sense of Personal Values and Motives for Action in a Management Context

Research into personal value's role in decisions and choices is marked by different operationalisations of personal values and decision-making, which makes comparisons between studies difficult. An emerging industry standard in personal values analysis is Schwartz's (1992) 10 universal values, in no particular order they are:

- *Self-Direction.* Independent thought and action; choosing, creating, exploring.
- *Stimulation.* Excitement, novelty, and challenge in life.
- *Hedonism.* Pleasure and sensuous gratification for oneself.

- *Achievement*. Personal success through demonstrating competence according to social standards.
- *Power*. Social status and prestige, control or dominance over people and resources.
- *Security*. Safety, harmony, and stability of society, of relationships, and of self.
- *Conformity*. Restraint of actions, inclinations, and impulses likely to upset or harm others and violate social expectations or norms.
- *Tradition*. Respect, commitment and acceptance of the customs and ideas that traditional culture or religion provide the self.
- *Benevolence*. Preserving and enhancing the welfare of those with whom one is in frequent personal contact (the 'in-group')
- *Universalism*. Understanding, appreciation, tolerance and protection for the welfare of all people and for nature.

They are referred to as universal values because Schwartz's (1992) work stems from cross-cultural research and have been found to be valid and reliable in every tested national culture. This cross-cultural element has increased its adoption to management research. Schwartz's (1992) values theory proposes that there are four higher-order motivational domains expressed as two bi-polar dimensional opposites: «Self-Transcendence vs. Self Enhancement» and «Openness to Change vs. Conservation».

Lichtenstein et al. (2017) compared and synthesised Schwartz's (1992) motivational domains to the major motivational theorists, including Maslow's (1987) theory of Sustenance Driven, Outer and Inner Directed Needs, and Deci and Ryan's (2008) Self-Determination Theory, illustrated in Fig. 2.3. The synthesis built upon values-based market research by CDSM Ltd. that was found in unpublished reports and subsequently replicated in a study of over 3,000 UK workers (Lichtenstein et al., 2015), found that Schwartz-based values data is congruent with Maslow (1987)-based values data. It became apparent that if you put Schwartz's (1992) values model and Deci and Ryan's (2008) Self-Determination Theory in a Maslovian dynamic (1987) all three theorists are essentially saying the same thing but in different ways.

This helps us understand personal values in the context of motivational domains, which gives rise to values orientations discussed below.

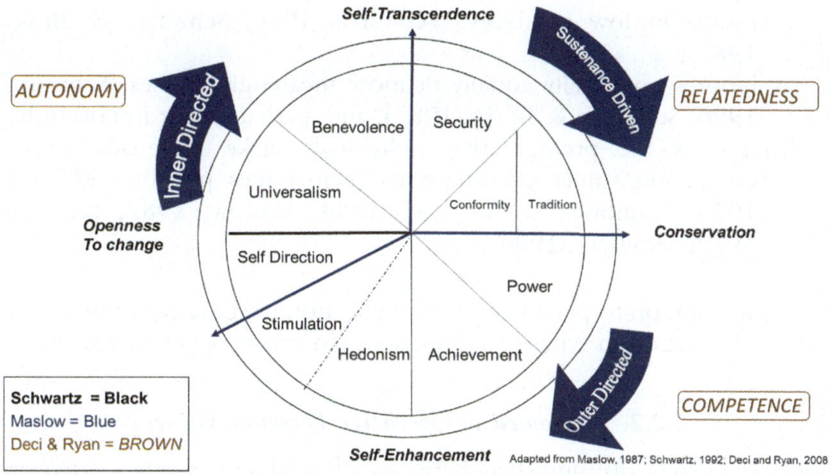

Fig. 2.3 Complementary motivational models (*Source* Lichtenstein et al. [2017])

2.2.1 Values Orientations

Although single values form a part of an individual's value system, a value system exists for each person that is organised in a system ordered by relative importance, as seen in the 10 value systems in the diagram above. Whilst there are personal values that are universally held in each culture, each individual will have a prominent set of values, "At the top of each person's system are a small handful of dominant values of paramount importance" (Hambrick & Brandon, 1988, p. 6), which are oriented towards underlying needs. England (1967, p. 54) defined a personal value system as 'a relatively' permanent perceptual framework that shapes and influences the general nature of an individual's behaviour'. As we will discuss and apply later in this chapter, one's values orientation is their motivational domain comprised of their lead values priorities that guide emotional states and choice behaviour, as seen in the outer ring of the circle in the diagram above. This is why research relying on only single values is inadequate, because by not considering one's values system or orientation it:

(i) results in low reliability (Schwartz, 1996; Schwartz & Bilsky, 1987),
(ii) ignores potentially equally or more meaningful values (Schwartz, 1996; Schwartz & Bilsky, 1987), and, perhaps most importantly,
(iii) ignores the premise that individuals make trade-offs among competing values according to their values priorities (Allport, 1955; Hambrick & Brandon, 1988; Maslow, 1987; Rokeach, 1979; Schwartz, 1996).

Before moving on to personal values application to strategy, we make one further distinction in types of values, adopted versus operative values.

2.2.2 *Adopted vs Operative Personal Values*

England (1967) distinguished between adopted values—those that are professed but not necessarily acted upon—and operative values—those that consistently guide behaviour, thus accounting for nuance and complexity in decision-making. In short, people with a dominant values orientation may make decisions at work that are reflective of alternative values orientations, based on a range of factors and possible consequences that are impossible to simulate outside of a work context (which many values studies do).

This difference between operative and adopted values is highlighted by the example of a high potential senior executive who several times a week 'walked-and-talked' the halls at work, greeting as many employees as possible while they worked. In her 360-degree assessment, subordinates and peers described her as cold and uncaring, shallow and self-centred. After hearing the comments, she agreed 100%. She explained that she did the 'walk the halls' only because it was an organisational requirement and that she didn't really care how the employees felt. Although we don't know the supervisor's personal values, using Fig. 2.3 we can make an educated guess it would be diametrically opposed to Benevolence and most probably in the Self enhancement/Outer Directed values orientation with Power and/or Achievement as her lead personal values. The takeaway is understanding people's operative versus espoused values is necessary to understand what's truly guiding them versus adopted values that are faked to 'get on'. We return to this point in Chapter 4 concerning strategy implementation.

With a brief introduction to personal values in a management context, the following sections explore its application to strategy.

2.3 Making Sense of the Personal Values-Strategic Choice Link

To make the conceptual applied, two further pieces of research are summarised as context for the mini cases in the personal values-strategy link that ends this chapter. The first is conceptual and the other is empirical.

2.3.1 How Value Systems Orientations Shape Value Creation

In a conceptual paper based on published and non-published personal values data, Lichtenstein and Dade (2007) proposed how the personal value orientations of strategic leaders influence their methods of creating value creation as seen in Table 2.1.

The conceptual development above laid the foundation for a further empirical study to investigate whether these values orientations manifest in predictable patterns of strategic decisions at work, outlined below. We will be returning to this table in the mini-case section.

Table 2.1 Proposed methods of creating shareholder value by executive values orientation

	Sustenance driven[a]/conservation	*Outer directed/self enhancement*	*Inner directed/self-transcendence*
Key executive values (Lichtenstein, 2005)	*Trust, Compassion, Affection, Loyalty*	*Prestige, Ambition, Power, Aggressiveness, Money*	*Innovation, Risk, Creativity, Autonomy*
Motto	If it ain't broke don't fix it	Be a winner	Make it novel
Vision	Tried and tested	Best practice	Innovation
Goal	Safe haven	Do things better	Do things differently
Strategy	Protect and defend	Second but better	First-to-market innovation

[a]Maslow's nomenclature
Source Adapted from Lichtenstein and Dade (2007)

2.3.2 *Personal Values at Work*

In contrast to prior research into personal values and strategic decision-making, Lichtenstein et al. (2017) investigated strategic decisions made in the workplace. If personal values shape decision-making, then the values orientation of decision-makers in an organisational context should be discernible in the decisions that they made thus confirm the role of personal values at work. The study explored whether executives' actual, job-related decision-making aligned with their values orientations.

In focus groups, strategic leaders with an Outer Directed (OD) or Inner Directed (ID) values orientation were prompted to reflect on their decisions at work. Analysis of the coded transcripts revealed the four independent raters reliably categorised coding events, according to a values orientation coding framework, which were statistically reliable. In other words, independently the coders were all seeing the same thing. Further statistical analysis found significant differences between executives' values orientation (ID or OD) and values decisions (ID or OD), demonstrating a consistent pattern of ID and OD decision-making. ID transcripts had significantly more ID codes than OD transcripts, and OD transcripts had statistically significantly more OD codes than ID transcripts did. The finding of statistically significant differences between the proportion of ID and OD comments in each set of their workplace decisions provided evidence that strategic leaders' choices are indeed reflected in their values orientations.

Qualitative analyses revealed a distinct pattern of responses that emerged across the two groups. Motives for action and strategic focus for ID respondents leaned towards intrinsic value, including *innovation*, *creativity*, *optimization* and *interdependency*. OD respondents leaned towards *company success*, including *efficiency*, *effectiveness*, *performance* and *winning*. Differences between the two values orientations are reflected in Table 2.2. For example, in Table 2.2, the ID manager in charge of successfully completing a project using a standard process, risks project failure and diminished company reputation on an untested product based solely on ID values related to *innovation*, *doing things differently* and *personal challenge*. In contrast, the OD executive reflects on a case in which managers at the highest level planned on not following through on a promise to pay bonuses if the work unit hit its performance target. The work unit hit the target, but upper management resisted paying the promised bonuses. The respondent's argument is not based

Table 2.2 Comments reflecting ID and OD values orientations

Inner-Directed (ID)	Outer-Directed (OD)
Intrinsic values, including *innovation, creativity, optimization* and *interdependency*	*Company success*, including *efficiency, effectiveness, performance* and *winning*
What motivates you at work? It's people. It's that whole interaction and dealing with people inspiring you, challenges. This point about dialogue is really important, and also for me it's really important to feel and touch the end product, the customer, whatever that product is and have a passion for it. It's fundamental	*What motivates you at work?* [T]he end goal for me is what you're happy to have in the organisation. That's my end goal irrespective of what the decision is—okay, at the end of the day how does this impact the organisation? Because that's my ultimate question, and if the answer's bad then don't do it. If it's good then do it
What motivates you to work harder? NG: To have the opportunity of primarily attacking new things, getting to know new people, to avoid a boring job KD: Yeah, doing things that are self-developing	*What motivates you to work harder?* There has to be clear leadership, clear focus and a clear direction, and I think once that's provided, how that's linked into what's being done on a daily basis. I think that there should be flexibility there, but as long as everybody knows where we're heading
Examples of values-based decisions and actions	
ID	OD
We had just started working with a new product…It's an IT product that's been developed by people within my company, but I have reservations about how successful it will be, so I'm quite concerned that it won't work. If it doesn't work, then this will be a huge failure, for me personally as well as the company. But if it does work, it's fantastic, a personal achievement	Towards the end of the financial year, my boss said to me, 'We're not going to give people as much money as we promised'…I said, 'Unfortunately if we do this, they're going to be demotivated. They're going to be upset…I would rather repay them what we promised them and you reduce my bonus, because at the end of the day if they don't work and they don't do the things they need to do, their problem is going to reflect on me'

ID: Inner-Directed; OD: Outer-Directed
Source Lichtenstein et al. (2017)

on ethics and justice in standing by a promise made. Rather, she expresses concern that the ramifications could result in decreased productivity that would reflect badly on her. For the OD executive, decisions are based primarily on organisational outcomes as a reflection of self.

This study established that there is a qualitative difference in the strategic decisions managers make by personal values orientations. Implications for researchers include advancing the efficacy of a behavioural strategy approach, support for Maslow's (1987) motivational theory and decision-making being consistent with personal values in an organisational context. Implications for practitioners include a predictable values-based pattern to managers' decisions and the need for a personal values-based leadership-strategy match, discussed in the following chapters.

Having reviewed the conceptual and some empirical underpinnings to the personal values strategic choice link, the next section introduces mini cases with questions for reflection.

2.4 Mini Cases in Personal Values-Strategy Link

One of the key messages of this pivot thus far is that our strategic decisions and choices are reflected in our personal values, whether we are conscious of them or not. If we want to gain emotional buy-in for strategy, it must be done at the level of personal values. Willingness to implement strategy only happens when strategy fits what one values (Updhyay et al., 2013). In strategic change, if people perceive that what they value is being ignored or being devalued, it will lead to resistance, resentment, rejection and/or repression. Whether trying to influence another person, a team or enterprise effective strategic leadership requires valuing the diversity of personal values in a team or organisation for strategy execution. The following section will explore mini-cases of both positive examples of buy-in and resistance in the context of a contextual framework.

2.4.1 The Values Dynamic & Congruence

The values dynamic—the dynamic between the personal values of the CEO and that of the workforce—is the crux of our understanding of a sustained value creation.

Lichtenstein and Dade (2007) offered a conceptual framework in Fig. 2.4 to illustrate this values dynamic. This shows that personal values are antecedents of vision, goals and strategy in service of creating value for stakeholders including the owners of the business. Concerning the stakeholder-value model, we refer to a chief executive's needs and values as Reality 1.1 because they are the lynchpin of the vision (Reality 2.0) and the existing culture (Reality 1.0). A guide to terminology and a mini-case study is provided to help illustrate the model.

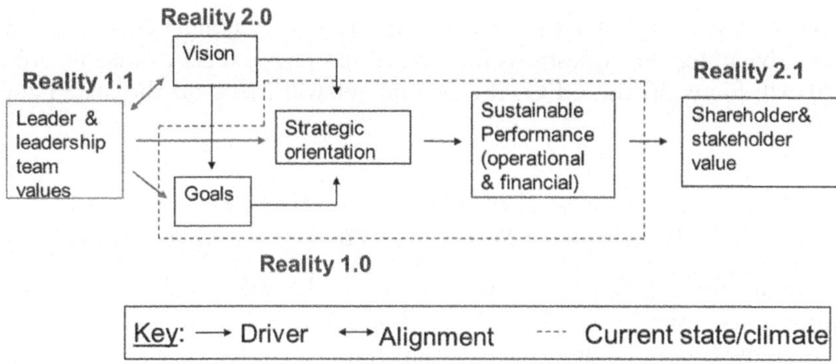

Fig. 2.4 The stakeholder value creation chain (*Source* Adapted from Lichtenstein and Dade [2007])

We call the dynamic between the personal values of the CEO and the leadership team with the rest of the organisation the values dynamic. Strategic leadership either creates or destroys value to the extent that it aligns Reality 1.0 with Reality 2.0. Individual CEOs/leaders on their own without followers can't create and sustain the strategic leadership required to align and shift an organisation: a vision that isn't shared can't engage emotional buy-in. Strategic leaders' values incongruence with the culture creates 'dis-ease', a sense at a fundamental level (that may even be difficult to articulate) that things aren't 'right'.

Sustained superior performance and value for stakeholders is achieved by chief executives and the leadership team achieving their desired ends through people. The dotted line in the model is what we refer to as the psychological climate.

The fit or similarity between the individual's personal values and what the organisation values is referred to as 'values congruence' (Lamm et al., 2010). Value congruence contends that individual behaviours within organisation are a result of interactions and subsequent fit between the organizational and personal characteristics including personal values (Chapman, 1991; House et al., 1996). When there is value congruence, the employee tends to be a good fit and give his best to the organisation (Zhang et al., 2008). Referring to conflict, McMurry (1963) stated that conflicts are fundamental differences at the level of personal values.

Below are mini case studies that explore values congruence and the values dynamic, with questions for reflection. The first set of case illustrations will focus on the CEO, the second set will focus on the leadership team.

2.4.2 CEO-Based Values Dynamic: Mini Cases in Values Alignment & Dis-Ease at Hewlett Packard and 3M

The values of leaders, particularly chief executive officers (CEOs), significantly impact employees (Upadhyay et al., 2013). The mini case illustrations below highlight the values dynamic and congruence with questions at the end.

2.4.3 Mini Case: Hewlett Packard

An example of values dynamic misalignment and alignment is briefly illustrated in this mini-case of ex-CEO Carly Fiorina's alignment of her vision for creating value at Hewett Packard (HP) in contrast to her successor Ex-CEO Mark Hurd. This case contrasts the dynamic between the leaders' values and that of the organisations and the impact on aligning or misaligning their methods of creating value with the culture.

Ex-CEO Carly Fiorina served as Chief Executive Officer and chairman of Hewlett-Packard from 1999 to 2005. In 2005, she was forced to resign following differences with the board of directors about how to execute HP's strategy. Ex-CEO Mark Hurd was CEO from March 2005 and resigned in August 2010. The company is renowned for its egalitarian, decentralised culture that came to be known as 'the HP Way.'[4]

[4] The HP Way was defined by co-founder Bill Hewlett as "a core ideology ... which includes a deep respect for the individual, a dedication to affordable quality and reliability, a commitment to community responsibility, and a view that the company exists to make technical contributions for the advancement and welfare of humanity." (Wikipedia) The following are the tenets of The HP Way:

We have trust and respect for individuals.
We focus on a high level of achievement and contribution.
We conduct our business with uncompromising integrity.
We achieve our common objectives through teamwork.
We encourage flexibility and innovation.

This involved one of the first all-company profit-sharing plans that gave shares to all employees, and offered tuition assistance, flex time and job sharing.

Research carried out by Waters (2008) into how leaders' values impact decision-making compared managers' perceptions of ex-CEO Carly Fiorina and ex-CEO Marc Hurd. Regarding Fiorina, a common perception amongst managers was that there was a values mismatch with the culture:

> People talked about the HP Way a lot and Carly came along and brushed that under the carpet a bit and people didn't like her for that. (Manager 1)

> I was never at all sure, other than her desire to be showbiz, quite what her values were. (Manager 2)

> With Carly Fiorina there were corporate values articulated and examples of things done by Carly which were disconnected, and I think that is what made a lot of people feel uncomfortable. (Manager 3)

In contrast, managers felt Mark Hurd did a far better job at aligning his method for creating value to the culture summarised by one manager:

> I do feel he (Mark Hurd) is more mapped to the basic core values of HP than Fiorina was; his wishes for operational tightness, profitability, and cost control are pretty much the same as the values fifty years ago. (Manager 4)

Questions

What was the values dynamic between Carly Fiorina and the then current culture of HP, Reality 1.0? Why was she creating dis-ease in the culture?

Now thinking about Mark Hurd, why was his values dynamic more successful?

You can be thinking about the lessons for strategic leaders trying to align their visions with goals, missions and strategies with the current workforce culture as you read the next mini case on 3M below.

2.4.4 Mini Case: 3M

The paper by Hind (2007) "At 3M, A struggle between Efficiency and Creativity" explains in-depth the changes wrought by McNerney and contrasts them with those made later by Buckley.

Prior to joining 3M in 2001, James McNerney competed with Bob Nardelli and Jeff Immelt to succeed the retiring Jack Welch as chairman and CEO of General Electric. When Immelt won the three-way succession race, McNerney left GE and joined 3M from 2001 to 2005, holding the position as chairman of the board and CEO. Sir George William Buckley was named chairman and CEO of 3M in December 2005 following the departure of McNerney who left abruptly to join Boeing. When McNerney joined, "he had barely stepped off the plane before he announced he would change the DNA of the place" (Hind, 2007, p. 1). McNerney began by implementing the GE play-book; axing 8,000 workers (about 11% of the workforce), intensifying the performance-review process, cutting spending and importing GE's Six Sigma programme—a series of management techniques designed to decrease production defects and increase efficiency. Thousands of staffers became trained as Six Sigma 'black belts'.

3M's creative culture that once gave rise to the 'Post It Note' phenomenon prided itself on drawing at least one-third of sales from products released in the past five years, and was underpinned by the '3M Way' that includes:

(i) Workers can seek out funding from a number of company sources to get their pet projects off the ground,
(ii) Official company policy allowing employees to use 15% of their time to pursue independent projects,
(iii) Ideas like the Post It Note are allowed to be fiddled with for several years before the product goes into full production, and.
(iv) The company explicitly encouraged risk and tolerated failure (Hind, 2007).

The focus on efficiency began driving out the innovation culture. Remembering a meeting at which technical employees were briefed on the new Six Sigma process, Michael Mucci, a 27-year veteran at 3 M recalls, "We all came to the conclusion that there was no way in the world that anything like a Post It Note would ever emerge from this new system"

(Hind, 2007, p. 2). The Post It Note inventor, 3M scientist Art Fry, reflecting on McNerney's culture change programme observed, "What's remarkable is how fast a culture can be torn apart. [McNerney] didn't kill it, because he wasn't here long enough. But if he had been here much longer, I think he could have" (Hind, 2007, p. 3).

Upon McNerney's departure, new CEO Buckley reinvigorated the workforce by reversing McNerney's legacy and getting back to the '3M Way' by scaling back on Six Sigma, boosting R&D spending, and rewarding risk taking. Reflecting on the process-focused approach of the past, Buckley remarked, "Perhaps one of the mistakes that we made as a company – it's one of the dangers of Six Sigma – is that when you value sameness more than you value creativity, I think you potentially undermine the heart and soul of a company like 3M" (Hind, 2007, p. 3). Tim Hammond, the director of strategic business development, states, "[Buckley] has brought back a spark around creativity." Bob Anderson, a business director in 3M's radio frequency identification division adds, "We feel like we can dream again" (Hind, 2007, p. 3). A contrast of the two leaders is found in Fig. 2.5.

Questions

From what you know about Sustenance Driven/Conservation, Outer Directed/Self Enhancement and Inner Directed/Self-Transcendence and

Fig. 2.5 A Tale of Two Leaders (*Source* Hind [2007])

Table 2.3 Proposed methods of creating shareholder value by executive values orientation

	Sustenance driven[a]/conservation[b]	*Outer directed/self enhancement*	*Inner directed/self-transcendence*
Motto	If it ain't broke don't fix it	Be a winner	Make it novel
Vision	Tried and tested	Best practice	Innovation
Goal	Safe haven	Do things better	Do things differently
Strategy	Protect and defend	Second but better	First-to-market innovation
On a Bumper sticker	Security, belonging	Success	Ideas

[a]Maslow's nomenclature
[b]Schwartz's nomenclature
Source Adapted from Lichtenstein and Dade (2007)

their preferred methods of creating value, can you infer the values orientations and strategy preferences of McNerny? Buckley? The previous Table 2.3 is reproduced to help you with the activity.

Think about the quote of the 3M inventor, "What's remarkable is how fast a culture can be torn apart."

- What is the values dynamic between James McNerney's personal values-Reality 1.1 and the then current culture of 3M, Reality 1.0? Why was McNerney's 'logical' playbook creating dis-ease in the culture?
- Now think about CEOs James Buckley's turnaround strategies and the 3M values dynamic
- Do you think he will be any more successful in creating long-term shareholder value? Why, or why not?
- What lessons can you draw for strategic leaders and what they need to reflect upon when trying to align their visions with goals, missions and strategies with the current workforce climate?

2.5 Summary

In this chapter, the link between personal values and strategy was investigated. Whilst the importance of personal values to strategic choice has been conceptually understood in strategy since the 1960s, the

Upper echelon theory provided the conceptual platform that subsequent research has built upon. Whilst personal values-based research in strategy is still at an early stage, there is growing empirical evidence that takes it out of the realm of merely conceptual. The relevance of the personal values-strategy link was discussed in the context of the values dynamic and values (in)congruence with mini case studies of Hewlett Packard and 3M to illustrate the how although personal values may seem like a 'woolly' concept, they are real and have practical consequences for managers and leadership. We move from the conceptual to the practical by having you construct your values story for buy-in based on the uncovering of your personal values.

Bibliography

Allport, G. W. (1955). *Becoming: Basic considerations for a psychology of personality*. Yale University Press.

Chapman, J. A. (1991). Matching people and organisations: Selection and socialization in public according firms. *Administrative Science Quarterly, 36*, 459–484.

Deci, E. L., & Ryan, R. M. (2008). Facilitating optimal motivation and psychological well-being across life's domains. *Canadian Psychology/psychologie Canadienne, 49*(1), 14–23.

England, G. W. (1967). Personal value systems of American managers. *Academy of Management Journal, 10*(1), 53–68.

England, G., & Lee, R. (1974). The relationship between managerial values and managerial success in the United States, Japan, India, and Australia. *Journal of Applied Psychology, 59*(4), 411–419.

Finkelstein, S., & D. Hambrick. (1996). *Strategic leadership: Top executives and their effects on organizations*. West Publishing Company.

Freeman, R. E., Gilbert, D. R., & Hartman, E. (1988). Values and the foundations of strategic management. *Journal of Business Ethics, 7*(11), 821–834.

Galavan, R., Kakabadse, A., & Kakabadse, N. (2003). The pivotal role of perceived discretion in top teams setting a research agenda. Conference Paper, British Academy of Management Conference, Harrogate.

Gupta, A. K., & Govindarajan, V. (1984). Business unit strategy, managerial characteristics, and business unit effectiveness at strategy implementation. *Academy of Management Journal, 27*, 25–41.

Hambrick, D. C. (2007). Upper echelons theory: An update. *Academy of Management Review, 32*(2), 334–343.

Hambrick, D. C., & Brandon, G. L. (1988). Executive Values. In D. C. Hambrick (Ed.), *The executive effect: Concepts and methods for studying top managers* (pp. 3–34). JAI Press.

Hambrick, D. C., & Mason, P. A. (1984). Upper echelons: The organization as a reflection of its top managers. *Academy of Management Review, 9*(2), 193–206.

Hind, B. (2007, June 11). *At 3M, a struggle between efficiency and creativity.* Bloomberg Businessweek.

House, R. J., Shane, S. A., & Herold, D. M. (1996). Rumors of the death of dispositional research are vastly exaggerated. *Academy of Management Review, 21*(1), 203–224.

Ismail, H. (2016). Preferences in business and corporate strategies: The role of personal values. *Contemporary Management Research, 12*(1), 25–45.

Lamm, E., Gordon, J. R., & Purser, R. E. (2010). The role of value congruence in organizational change. *Organization Development Journal, 28*(2), 49.

Lawrence, B. S. (1997). Perspective—The black box of organizational demography. *Organization Science, 8*(1), 1–22.

Lewin, K. (1951). Field theory in social science: selected theoretical papers (D. Cartwright, Ed.). Harper & Row.

Lichtenstein, S. (2005). *Strategic Co-alignment: Strategic, Executive values and organisational Goal orientation and their Impact on Performance* (DBA thesis). Henley Management College/Brunel University

Lichtenstein, S., & Dade, P. (2007). The shareholder value chain: Values, vision and shareholder value creation. *Journal of General Management, 33*(1), 15–31.

Lichtenstein, S., Higgs, M., & Samuel, P. (2015) *Can Employee Values Predict Work Behaviour?* British Academy of Management. Conference Paper.

Lichtenstein, S., Lichtenstein, G., & Higgs, M. (2017). Personal values at work: A mixed-methods study of executives' strategic decision-making. *Journal of General Management, 43*(1), 15–23.

Ling, Y., Zhao, H., & Baron, R. A. (2007). Influence of founder—CEOs' personal values on firm performance: Moderating effects of firm age and size. *Journal of Management, 33*(5), 673–696.

Maslow, A. H. (1987). *Motivation and personality* (3rd ed., R. Frager, J. Fadiman, C. McReynolds, & R. Cox, Eds.). Harper & Row

McMurry, R. N. (1963). Conflicts in human-values. *Harvard Business Review, 41*(3), 130.

Miller, D., Kets de Vries, M. F., & Toulouse, J. M. (1982). Top executive locus of control and its relationship to strategy-making, structure, and environment. *Academy of Management Journal, 25*(2), 237–253.

Morris, M. H., & Davis, D. L. (1994). Fostering corporate entrepreneurship: Cross-cultural comparisons of the importance of individualism versus collectivism. *Journal of International Business Studies, 25*, 65–89.

Nightingale, D. V., & Toulouse, J. M. (1977). Toward a multilevel congruence theory of organization. *Administrative Science Quarterly*, 264–280.

Pettigrew, A. (1992). On studying managerial elites. *Strategic Management Journal, 13*, 163–182.

Pfeffer, J. (1983). Organizational demography. In B. Staw & L. Cummings (Eds.), *Research in organizational behaviour* (Vol. 5, pp. 299–357). JAI Press.

Postman, L., Bruner, J. S., & McGinnies, E. (1948). Personal values as selective factors in perception. *The Journal of Abnormal and Social Psychology, 43*(2), 142–154.

Rokeach, M., (1979). From Individual to Institutional Values: With Special Reference to the Values of Science. In M. Rokeach (Ed.), *Understanding human values: Individual and societal* (pp. 47–70). Free Press.

Rothschild, W. E. (1993). *Risktaker, caretaker, surgeon, undertaker: The four faces of strategic leadership*. John Wiley & Sons Inc.

Schwartz, S. (1992). Universals in the content and structure of values: Theoretical advances and empirical test in 20 countries. In M. P. Zannam (Ed.), *Advances in experimental social psychology* (Vol. 25, pp. 1–65). Academic Press.

Schwartz, S. (1996). Value Priorities and Behavior: Applying a Theory of Integrated Value Systems. In C. Seligman, J. M. Olson, & M. P. Zanna (Eds.), *The psychology of values: The Ontario Symposium* (Vol. 8). Lawrence Erlbaum

Schwartz, S. H., & Bilsky, W. (1987). Toward a theory of the universal content and structure of values: Extensions and cross-cultural replications. *Journal of Personality and Social Psychology, 58*(5), 878.

Schyns, B., & Felfe, J. (2006). The personality of followers and its effect on the perception of leadership: An overview, a study, and a research agenda. *Small Group Research, 37*(5), 522–539.

Szilagyi Jr, A. D., & Schweiger, D. M. (1984). Matching managers to strategies: A review and suggested framework. *Academy of Management Review, 9*(4), 626–637.

Thomas, A. S., Lichert, R., & Ramaswamy, K. (1991). The performance impact of strategy – manager coalignment: An empirical examination. *Strategic Management Journal, 12*, 509–522.

Thomas, A. S., & Ramaswamy, K. (1996). Matching managers to strategy: Further tests of the Miles and Snow typology. *British Journal of Management, 7*, 247–261.

Upadhyay, A. Y. A., Upadhyay, A. K., & Palo, S. (2013). Strategy implementation using balanced scorecard: Achieving success through personal values of leaders and employees. *Management and Labour Studies, 38*(4), 447–469.

Waters, M. (2008). *Leadership values* (MBA Dissertation). Henley Management College/Brunel University.

Zhang, X., Austin, S., Glass, J., & Mills, G. (2008). Toward collective organizational values: A case study in UK construction. *Construction Management and Economics, 26*(10), 1009–1028.

CHAPTER 3

Developing Strategy Based on Personal Values

Abstract This chapter explores the key components in devising a values-guided strategy employing the strategy-as-values congruence approach. Following the discussion of values-guided strategy as a social influencing process, we introduce a tool to help you discover your personal values with guiding questions to facilitate the development of your values-guided strategy. This is done in the context of strategy as storytelling that covers the ingredients for a strategy-as-story approach for emotional buy-in from key internal and external stakeholders. Personal values aligned strategy in action is illuminated by a mini case of a senior manager in the financial services sector, 'Alex', and his personal values-guided career transition. Finally, a mini case study 'Taking the Bull by the Horns' unpacks valued-guided strategy in the context of the leadership team values dynamics from the most successful coach in US professional Basketball history to with questions for managers and leaders to reflect upon devising and getting buy-in for values-guided strategy alignment.

Keyword Social influencing process · Strategy as storytelling · Personal values congruence · Leadership team values · Intellectual and emotional buy-in

S. Lichtenstein and M. Higgs, *Strategy through Personal Values*,
https://doi.org/10.1007/978-3-030-88269-3_3

3.1 Strategy as Personal Values Congruence/Alignment

The strategy-as-values-congruence perspective argues that strategic leaders' primary concern should be to identify their personal values, which moves them (Lichtenstein, 2001). Secondly, strategic leaders should be focusing actively on any changes needed in the organisation's values proposition, in order to achieve a better match with the aspirations of employees and other key internal and external stakeholders including customers. Having done this, the key to emotional buy-in is translating the organisation's purpose, goals and strategies into the operative personal values of direct reports and employees, a theme we develop in Chapter 4. Emotional buy-in is the crux of getting commitment from internal and external stakeholders to a strategy, and therefore central to implementation, which is discussed further below.

A key component in the strategy-as-values-match perspective is the fit between corporate values and the aspirations of employees. It is thought that this 'fit' is integral to the establishment of a distinct and shared corporate identity. Such an identity can confer on a company strategy a potential source of competitive advantage that cannot be easily copied and, at the same time, establish employee emotional commitment or buy-in to such a strategy. The opportunity to raise organisational effectiveness through logical and emotional attachment between employee and company is implicit in the congruence between employees' and leader's values.

Personal values as guiding principles in life that shape choices and behaviour are at the crux of sense-making (Hitlin & Pinkston, 2013; Robinson, 2015; Schwartz & Bilsky, 1987; Tsirogianni & Gaskell, 2011). Whether we are conscious of them or not, personal values filter our perception of the industry, the organisation underpinning the evaluative judgements along the strategy journey, as illustrated in Fig. 3.1.

3.1.1 Sense Making/Giving

By uncovering patterns in the whole organisational system, the strategy-as-values-alignment approach can help develop sense-making leadership capacity. At the core of strategy as a practice is to make sense of the organisational situation an individual, team or business unit is in, and then to give that sense to stakeholders, known collectively as 'sense make/give'.

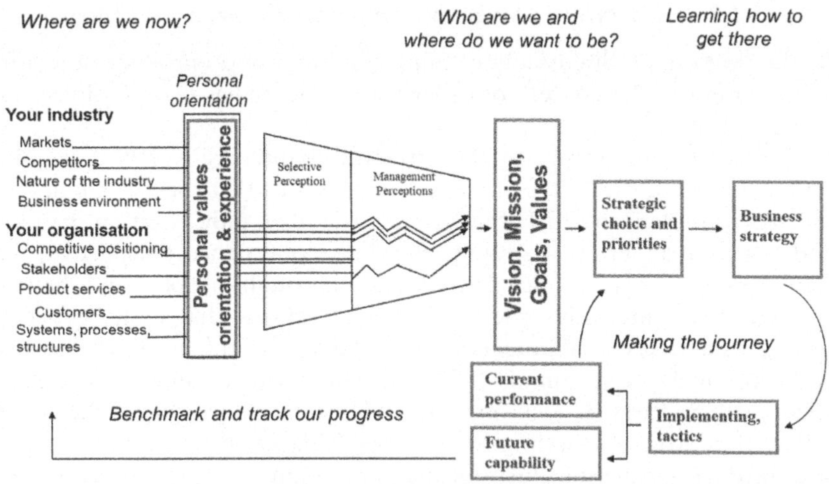

Fig. 3.1 Personal values-guided strategy (*Source* Adapted from Hughes and Beatty [2005] and Hambrick and Mason [1984])

Sense-making is the capability to see what's happening on the surface and to understand the root cause before attempting to solve the problem or bring about change (Aitken & Higgs, 2010). This ability to recognise, understand and address what is going on as a whole system is a practice and key capability of any informal and formal leader wanting to make lasting change (Aitken & Higgs, 2010). Sense-make/give capability allows a greater awareness and understanding of the dynamics underpinning inter-personal and organisational life, to diagnose root causes to devise and implement strategies for lasting change that closes the performance gap between where we are now and where we 'ought' to be.

The next sections cover what values-guided strategy is, namely a social influencing process of gaining intellectual and emotional buy-in. Conceiving it as a process differs from traditional ways of seeing strategy.

3.1.2 *The 6th 'P': Strategy as a Social Influencing Process*

In this section we discuss values-guided strategy and enrolling others in its execution in the context of other ways strategy has been traditionally conceived of.

There are many ways to define strategy, Mintzberg's (1987) seminal article regarding the 5 'P's of strategy reminds us that there is a plurality of ways to understand it. It can be seen as a plan, ploy, position, pattern and perspective. From a strategy-as-values congruence perspective, we view strategy as achieving desired ends through people, and hence, strategy is an interactive social influencing *process* that exists between strategists and key stakeholders that impacts upon the emotion (hearts) and sense-make/give (minds) of those who assent to and implement it (Parry, 1998; Parry & Jackson, 2016). Personal values colour the social influencing process including the nature of relationships, communication and information sharing. Just putting your common-sense hat on, would a strategic leader who craves *Control* versus one who craves *Creativity* have different types of relationships, ways of communicating and share information differently'? Of course! They would even dress and drive differently. Therefore, understanding what moves ourselves and others is a key leadership skill. Effective strategic leaders' practice and build the leadership capability of *Personal values sensitivity*, defined as tuning into all the interests, beliefs and motivational drivers present in important communication and interaction, starting with your own (McKenzie & Aitken, 2012).

The next section on uncovering your own values aims to help you build personal values sensitivity. Understanding your own values is the first step in building personal values sensitivity.

The next section discusses potential blocks to aligning people to strategy as well as key concepts in the acceptance and commitment to execute strategy.

3.1.3 *To What End? Intellectual and Emotional Buy-In*

Devising strategy is inextricably wed to getting intellectual and emotional buy-in for it. As we'll see in the mini-case at the end of the chapter 'Taking the Bull by the horns', a strategy without buy-in is a delusion; the team has to own it, and if they do, terrific success can result. If those implementing the strategy sense what they value isn't being valued or the strategy is seen as a threat, employees engage in defensive routines they can resist the strategy, and over time that resistance can build into resentment (Argyris, 1985). Argyris (1985) describes defensive routines as actions that are designed to protect individuals and groups to deal with a threatening environment to reduce pain that simultaneously inhibits learning. What Argyris (1985) found was rather than openly resisting a strategy or an intolerable boss, the mislabelled 'subordinates' comply and salute whilst at the same time suppressing their frustrations and anger. A self-reinforcing cycle can occur whereby there is an acceptance of demands (e.g. to implement the strategy with a secret rejection of the demands for execution that becomes undiscussable).

Resentment can 'stack' on top of resentment and building up over time, just like it does in a bad relationship. Left to fester, resentment can lead to rejection of the strategy and even sabotage. Resentment over time can lead to repression just like couples in a dysfunctional relationship that never talk to each other. This underlying dynamic may in part explain the high levels of global employee disengagement. According to Gallup's (2020) engagement survey 63% of the workforce are not engaged, i.e., they are not emotionally invested and focused on creating value for their organisations, and 24% are actively disengaged, meaning they are emotionally disconnected from their workplaces and less likely to be productive. Why not nip resistance in the bud before it builds into resentment and so create a healthy climate for strategy implementation?

3.1.3.1 Intellectual Buy-In

Intellectual buy-in refers to understanding what the strategy and what desired ends are. One of the main barriers to employees' buy-in to strategy is confusion about terminology (Callander, 2020). If employees don't know what the objectives and strategy are, they ask themselves, 'Where do I fit in?' More importantly, without shared sense-making amongst followers those tasked with implementation aren't able to respond and take action. A lack of understanding is the enemy of intellectual buy-in and execution, but taking action requires something else.

3.1.3.2 Emotional-Buy-In

Emotional buy-in is a commitment and willingness to execute. The crux of emotional buy-in is aligning strategy to what people already value at the level of their personal values. When this happens there is a psychological ownership stake in the strategy's success. When emotional buy-in at the level of personal values is engaged, execution follows. After all, what is emotion but energy-directed motion? To put it simply, strategy without a commitment at the level of personal values is a delusion.

Robinson's (2015) research into acceptance or resistance to change found that the resonance of personal values preferences was the key determinant in responses to strategies for change. She found that senior managers are inclined to approve change strategies when the idea resonates with their values priorities and motivational goals and disapprove change when perceived as an affront to their personal values. In other words, people don't resist new strategies and change: they resist losing what they value (Latting & Ramsey, 2009). So, the key to emotional buy-in is values alignment: aligning the underlying values people wish to protect and preserve and aligning it to the strategy (Latting & Ramsey, 2009). This is discussed in more detail in Chapter 4.

The next section moves from the conceptual to the applied by introducing a tool for personal values discovery. Uncovering your own values is the first step in developing personal values sensitivity

3.2 Discovering Your Own Personal Values at Work Self-Assessment: Explorers, Enterprisers and Settlers

Successful personal values-guided strategists understand what moves themselves and others. Most of us misguidedly assume what guides our discretionary performance also motivates others. Is it any wonder our record on sustaining performance and profitability is so patchy and inconsistent?

If you have completed a personal values inventory previously, please use it to complement the results from the below.

3.2.1 Personal Values Self-Assessment

Based on a synthesis of quantitative and qualitative research and personal values-based coaching we've constructed a personal values self-assessment tool to facilitate a deep dialogue and reflection to uncover the silent power of your values. It complements the Personal Orientation Survey which is an online personal values instrument and reporting tool.

Based on motives for action, personal values orientation-based research and values items from Schwartz (1992, 1994), a typology for values-guided strategy is introduced below using the three personal values orientations of Settlers, Enterprisers and Explorers as seen in Fig. 3.2.

Below is the detail of each of the three values orientations. Please rate the values using the scale provided and sub-total each section. You'll be asked to tally the sub-sections, transfer them to the assessment sheet and convert them into percentages at the end to uncover your lead values system and orientation. The results of your values orientation can then be linked to strategy preferences.

Only you can ultimately decide what your true personal values are, but hopefully this self-assessment is a useful tool for dialogue and reflection.[1] In devising your values-guided strategy it's recommended to review your strongest highest scoring value(s) and your weakest lowest scoring value(s). What's influenced your strongest values? Where did they come from? Think of illustrations and anecdotes that exemplify these values.

Below are some questions that may help you create your values-guided strategy:

> In what ways do personal values show up for you in your work life? Have you noticed any values that have changed either personal or societal? Have you let go of certain values or adopted new ones? What are the consequences of our personal values for your strategic leadership challenges?

The next section contextualises your results of the Personal Values Self-Assessment tool to devise your values-based strategy as a story. Communicating your values-guided strategy as a story will increase buy-in from internal and external stakeholders.

3.3 Getting Buy-In for Strategy: Your Strategy as Story

An effective way to get buy-in for your values-guided strategy is to understand strategy as storytelling. Strategy stories express the creative capacity of an individual, team or organisation, its emotions, identities,

[1] The Personal Orientation Survey on-line instrument, reporting tool and debrief can add further insight available at: scottl@evsconsulting.co.uk.

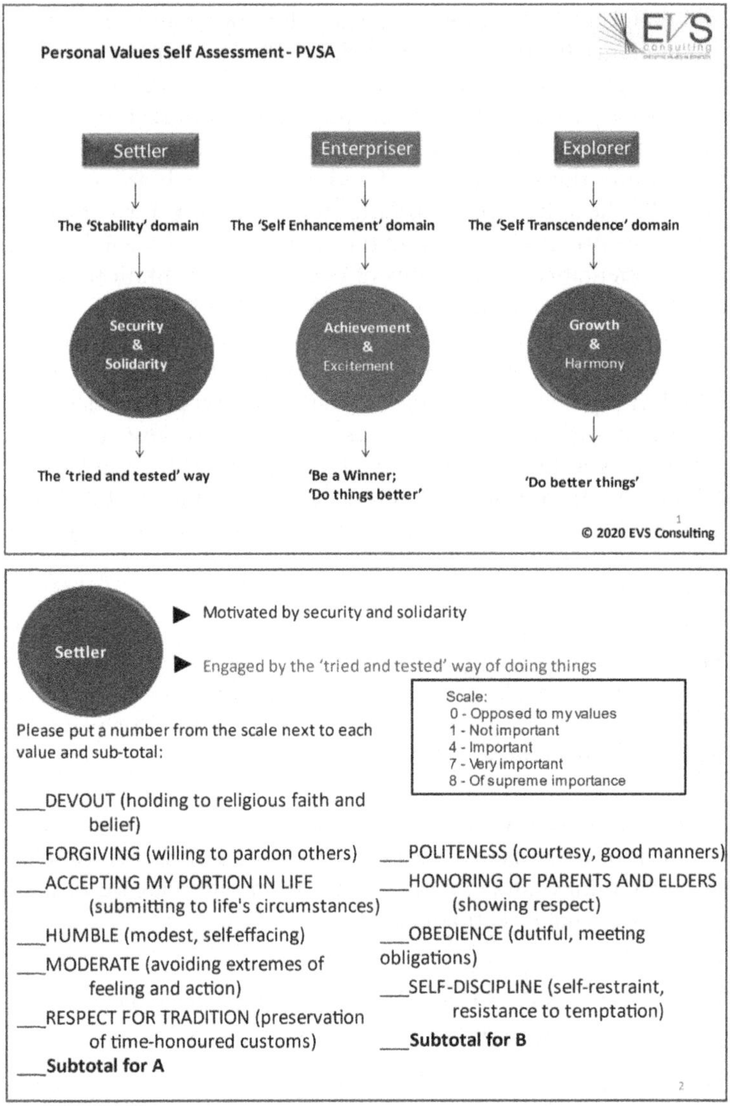

Fig. 3.2 Personal values self-assessment

Settler

▶ Motivated by security and solidarity

▶ Engaged by the 'tried and tested' way of doing things

Scale:
0 - Opposed to my values
1 - Not important
4 - Important
7 - Very important
8 - Of supreme importance

Please put a number from the scale next to each value and total at the bottom:

___CLEAN (neat, tidy)
___NATIONAL SECURITY (protection of my nation from my enemies)
___ SOCIAL ORDER (stability of society)
___FAMILY SECURITY (safety for loved ones)
___RECIPROCATION OF FAVORS (avoidance of indebtedness)
___SENSE OF BELONGING (feeling that others care about me)
___**Subtotal for C**

___**Total Score (A+B+C)**

Enterpriser

▶ Motivated by Achievement, and wanting it all-now

▶ Engaged by Winning and novelty

Scale:
0 - Opposed to my values
1 - Not important
4 - Important
7 - Very important
8 - Of supreme importance

Please put a number from the scale next to each value and total at the bottom:

___SOCIAL POWER (control over others, dominance)
___AUTHORITY (the right to lead or command)
___WEALTH (material possessions, money)
___PRESERVING MY PUBLIC IMAGE (protecting my "face")
___SOCIAL RECOGNITION (respect, approval by others)
___**Subtotal D**

___SUCCESSFUL (achieving goals)
___CAPABLE (competent, effective, efficient)
___AMBITIOUS (hard working, aspiring)
___INFLUENTIAL (having an impact on people and events)
___INTELLIGENT (logical, thinking
___SELF RESPECT (belief in one's own worth)
___**Subtotal E**

Fig. 3.2 (continued)

Enterpriser

▶ Motivated by Achievement, and wanting it all-now

▶ Engaged by Winning and novelty

Scale:
0 - Opposed to my values
1 - Not important
4 - Important
7 - Very important
8 - Of supreme importance

Please put a number from the scale next to each value and total at the bottom:

___ENJOYING LIFE (enjoying food, sex, leisure, etc.)

___PLEASURE (gratification of desires)

___Subtotal F

___DARING (seeking adventure, risk)

___A VARIED LIFE (life filled with challenge, novelty and change)

___AN EXCITING LIFE (stimulating experiences)

___Subtotal G

___FREEDOM of action

___INDEPENDENT (self reliant, self sufficient)

___Subtotal H

___Total Score (D+E+F+G+H)

5

Explorer

▶ Motivated by growth and contribution

▶ Engaged by purpose and the journey

Scale:
0 - Opposed to my values
1 - Not important
4 - Important
7 - Very important
8 - Of supreme importance

Please put a number from the scale next to each value and total at the bottom:

__FREEDOM of thought

__CREATIVITY (uniqueness, imagination)

__CURIOUS (interested in everything, exploring)

___CHOOSING OWN GOALS (selecting own purposes)

___Subtotal I

___A WORLD OF BEAUTY (beauty of nature and the arts)

___PROTECTING THE ENVIRONMENT (preserving nature)

(Continued)

___UNITY WITH NATURE (fitting into nature)

___BROAD-MINDED (tolerant of different ideas and beliefs)

___SOCIAL JUSTICE (correcting injustice, care for the weak)

___WISDOM (a mature understanding of life)

___EQUALITY (equal opportunity for all)

___A WORLD AT PEACE (free of war and conflict)

___INNER HARMONY (at peace with myself)

___Subtotal J

6

Fig. 3.2 (continued)

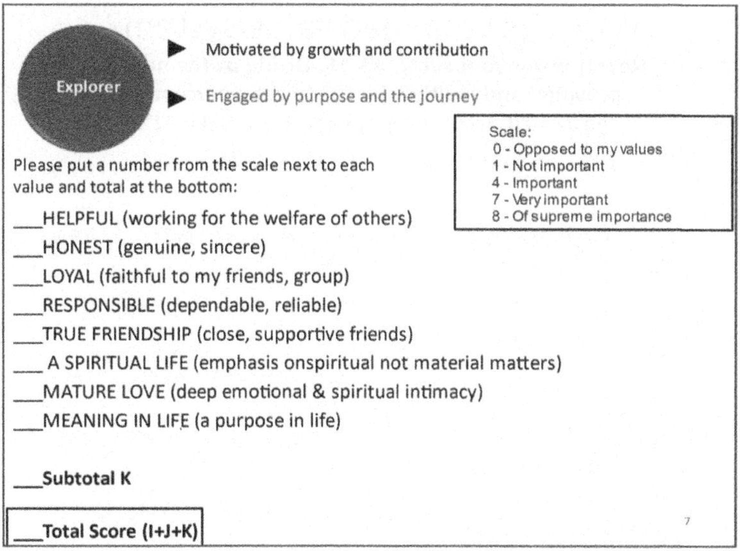

Explorer

▶ Motivated by growth and contribution

▶ Engaged by purpose and the journey

Scale:
0 - Opposed to my values
1 - Not important
4 - Important
7 - Very important
8 - Of supreme importance

Please put a number from the scale next to each value and total at the bottom:

___HELPFUL (working for the welfare of others)
___HONEST (genuine, sincere)
___LOYAL (faithful to my friends, group)
___RESPONSIBLE (dependable, reliable)
___TRUE FRIENDSHIP (close, supportive friends)
___ A SPIRITUAL LIFE (emphasis onspiritual not material matters)
___MATURE LOVE (deep emotional & spiritual intimacy)
___MEANING IN LIFE (a purpose in life)

___Subtotal K

___Total Score (I+J+K)

7

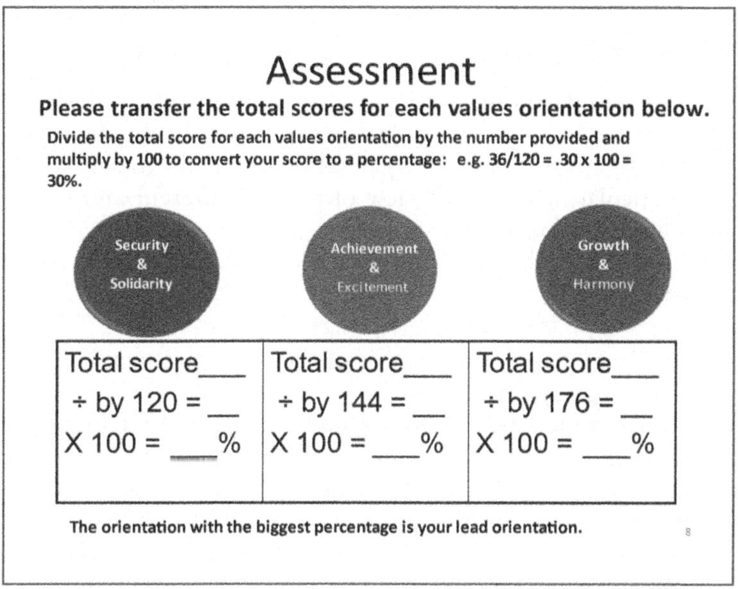

Assessment

Please transfer the total scores for each values orientation below.

Divide the total score for each values orientation by the number provided and multiply by 100 to convert your score to a percentage: e.g. 36/120 = .30 x 100 = 30%.

Security & Solidarity	Achievement & Excitement	Growth & Harmony
Total score___ ÷ by 120 = __ X 100 = ___%	Total score___ ÷ by 144 = __ X 100 = ___%	Total score___ ÷ by 176 = __ X 100 = ___%

The orientation with the biggest percentage is your lead orientation.

8

Fig. 3.2 (continued)

Which is your lead value system?

Now transfer your subtotals A-K. Divide by the number provided and multiply by 100 to get a percentage.
e.g.A = 20_Tradition ÷ by 48 = .417 x 100 = 42%.

A = ___**Tradition**÷ by 48 = ___
x 100 = ___%

B = ___**Conformity**÷ by 32 = ___
x 100 = ___%

C = ___**Security**÷ by 48 = ___
x 100 = ___%

D = ___**Power**÷ by 40 = ___
x 100 = ___%

E = ___**Achievement**÷ by 48 = ___
x 100 = ___%

F = ___**Hedonism** ÷ by 16 = ___
x 100 = ___ %

G = ___ **Stimulation** ÷ by 21 = ___ x 100
= ___%

H = ___ **Self Direction** ÷ by 16 = ___ x
100 = ___%

I = ___ **Self Explore** ÷ by 32 = ___ x 100
= ___%

J = ___ **Universalism** ÷ by 72 = ___ x 100
= ___%

K = ___ **Benevolence** ÷ by 64 = ___ x 100
= ___%

The largest percentage is your lead value system

9

Fig. 3.2 (continued)

understandings and actions (Downing, 1999). Storytelling, therefore, is a powerful way to give sense to internal and external stakeholders about the logic of how the individual and organisation competes to achieve desired ends. In particular, it's a linked view of the past, present and future that gives meaning to values-based strategy.

As opposed to 'talk' or 'spin', this approach is rooted in the sense make/give approach:

(i) effective managers spend most of their working time listening and talking anyway (Hales, 2007),
(ii) effective leaders listen to stakeholder issues and integrate them in a story/vision (Reich, 1987),
(iii) Learning organisations stimulate discussions about means and shared values as ends (Pascale, 1990). Pascale (1990) argues that senior managers at Honda were able to promote dialogue and work as listeners and facilitators to channel differing opinions into one plan,
(iv) Competitive advantage is based on communicating across functions (Prahalad & Hamel, 1990). In their seminal article "The

Core Competence of the Corporation" they observed, "Core competence is communication, involvement and a deep commitment to working across boundaries. It involves many levels of people and all functions" (Prahalad & Hamel, 1990, pp. 256–259). Kay (1995) referred to this as 'social architecture',

(v) Intellectual capital grows when networks share language and narratives (Nahapiet & Ghoshal, 1998). These forms of communications when shared assists the creation of new knowledge and ways of working.

Management and strategy are therefore, a relational process that effective strategists are part of and facilitate. Influencing relationships to engender trust and goodwill will no doubt become even a more important part of the strategist's job.

3.3.1 Narrative

Thinking of your strategy as a narrative will help internal and external stakeholders make sense of your strategy story. A narrative structure is the means by which we recognise a story, the simplest being a beginning, middle and an end. A narrative could include at least these 5 elements (Downing, 1999):

- Endpoints or goals
- Key actions relevant to the goal
- A chronology linking these events,
- A cause-and-effect logic linking the key events to the goals, and
- Milestones or endings which show the achievement or failure to achieve the goals.

These elements allow stakeholders to rationalise the strategy that allows them to elaborate on in its re-telling a particular context or situation.

3.3.2 Storylines

Storylines are stories that are remembered and repeated such as what's 'hot' and what's not that conveys particular points for a particular audience or context. Storylines evoke emotions—positive or negative—including feelings of satisfaction, happiness, anger, sadness or being afraid

(Barry & Elmes, 1997). As strategies are never value-free, it's worth asking what are the storylines that underpin the narrative? For example, are there storyline themes that include perceptions of *fairness* or *equality* (e.g. the humanity of the boss or offering), *security*, making progress on problems/problem solving, comparisons with other companies or obstacles in achieving the desired ends?

The organisation's strategy narrative may be part of a larger plot or storyline being shared by other stakeholders. A plot is an abstract, generic pattering or structure of action that provides a frame of reference for stakeholders to situate their rational and emotional understanding (Toolan, 2012). In a sense, receivers of the story will be trying to sense the plot in organisational action.

Below are four common plots that derive from romantic, melodramatic, ironic and tragic literature summarised below in Table 3.1.

Managers also need to be aware of how they and their strategies are being perceived by different stakeholders. The Quest plot is how we would like our strategies to be perceived, any setbacks seen as part of a longer progressive journey. This plot engenders trust and support for strategy, whereas the emergence of other plots engender mistrust, and hence, the need for feedback loops to know what stories stakeholders are saying.

In developing strategies as narratives and storylines, it is worth noting other stakeholders may well be developing their own competing stories about the strategy narrative. For example, senior managers may wish to communicate an acquisition strategy as a *Quest* to increase market share

Table 3.1 Four common plots

The Quest (Romance)	The Downfall (Tragedy)	The Contest (Melodrama)	The Scam (Irony)
A progressive hero-adventurer challenges the status quo or conventional wisdom, experiences setbacks, but ultimately succeeds	A hero is pitched from success to danger and humiliation, primarily as a result of fate or external events	Where a polarised struggle between two heroes characterised as good and evil, leads to a battle in which the opposition is defeated	Where a hero is exposed as incompetent, corrupt or a fool; apparently heroic actions are re-interpreted as a scam to fleece others

Source Adapted from Downing (1999)

and entry into new marks, opportunities for more training, improved customer satisfaction and consequently boosting earnings per share. However, employees may see it as a *Contest* and link it with job losses and a poorly conceived attempt to merge two antagonistic cultures of rival companies. The media may view it as a *Scam* and link it to board-room excess, reduction in competition and consumer choice (Downing, 1999).

Whilst the big story of plots may be out of the control of strategists, the narrative and storylines of a strategy can engender buy-in by being memorable and repeated. The narrative structure is a means by which to create compelling storylines to create a simplified and rationalised story.

Going back to where the chapter started, if strategists present visions without attending to stakeholders' contexts of what is, the gap between Reality 1.0 and 2.0 may be seen as incredible and potentially a *scam*. If the buy-in is not achieved and attended to, anger in the form of resistance can result and lead to a melodramatic contest amongst some stakeholders. Strategists would do well to remember a sense of satisfaction by internal and external customers and other stakeholders are necessary to gain support for strategy as *quest*.

3.3.3 What's Your Strategy Story?

Reflecting on your values-guided strategy, initiative or behaviour how you might incorporate the elements of strategy as storytelling? Think of your or your team's, division, strategic business unit (SBU) or company's strategy as a values-guided story. What's the narrative? Are there key storylines or themes that support the narrative?

Are there plots which internal and external stakeholders are retelling about the organisation's strategy? How do they fit into your narrative?

In developing your values-guided strategy you can reflect on the narrative, key storylines or themes that support it.

The next section examines values alignment strategies in action, personal and team based.

3.4 Personal Values Alignment in Action: The Mini Case of Alex

Some may find organisational strategy abstract, particularly if one isn't directly involved in formulating it. However, we can all relate to a time we made values-guided decisions that shaped our destiny: who to work with and who not to work with, when to give our discretionary performance above and beyond pay and conditions and when not to. As you read this mini case you can be thinking of a time when your personal values came into play in a work context, and the extent to which you accepted or rejected particular organisational pressures.

The mini case below of Alex is based on case studies of executives in the financial services sector carried out by Emma Watton at Lancaster University discussed in a paper by Lichtenstein et al. (2016) exploring the role of personal values winning out over organisational values when managers face ethical dilemmas. This case of Alex below illustrates how formally and informally recognised leader's alignment and legacy are shaped by their personal values priorities.

As we have stressed through this book, effective strategic leaders need to understand what moves them and others: how their needs and personal values shape their decisions and how these decisions shape their destinies. These decisions are reflected in our moral and ethical stances with consequences for one's own strategic leadership 'brand' and ultimately the legacy we leave.

3.4.1 Alex

We first met Alex in 2012. At the time he was Executive Vice President for Global Sales at a financial services corporation that we will refer to as Emergent Solutions. The company develops software service technology for the financial services industry. The company has a global reach of more than 300 employees. Alex has been with the company for 7 years and has 13 years of industry experience. The company has rapidly expanded in recent years, growing from fewer than 50 employees to more than 300. Much of this growth has been due to acquisitions of other firms in the same market. Six acquisitions have occurred over the last five years.

Due to scrutiny increasingly faced by companies in the financial services industry, Alex shared with us insights about how his company's culture, its leadership, and organisational processes have changed following the global financial crisis in 2007/2008. Describing the recruitment strategy of the company Alex said, “So what we try to do is find innovative young people who are still at the start of their career and willing to take risks”.

In terms of organisational goals and personal alignment, Alex commented, “We haven’t nailed that one yet; it’s one of our biggest challenges. We have to make sure that the objectives and goals of the managing directors are aligned with the executive vice president group and all other employees.” Alex expanded on this point highlighting what might happen if there were misalignment or non-conformist behaviour. “If someone’s behaviour is consistently against the flow of what we are trying to achieve, then we will just agree that this is not working out and there has got to be a better place where this person has a better fit. So we are not going to tolerate behaviour that is not aligned with what we want to achieve on an on-going or consistent basis.”

Talking about bonus and performance management Alex explained, “We provide stock and cash bonuses for ideas that result in significant business growth. So if someone leads us to an acquisition or a new channel partnership development deal like a re-seller, we compensate them handsomely for that…activity that obviously enriches the business.”

Fast forward to 2016. Alex doesn’t work in the financial services industry anymore. He decided to co-fund a not-for-profit company in 2011 and joined it full-time as a board director in 2014. The company describes itself as a social impact organisation and employs a handful of core staff and has a large number of volunteers who help the company to deliver a diverse range of community projects. Alex describes the company as “good for my soul and it means I can give back”.

This might at first seem strange given Alex’s former success as a senior leader in an expanding global business. Alex confided in us, “I turned my back on a stellar career and I decided I don’t want this anymore. There were many reasons why, including searching for self-fulfillment and giving something back but, I also disliked a lot of what I saw in the industry: a lack of honesty, a lack of integrity, a lack of transparency.”

Before making this decision, Alex asked some searching questions. He reflected, “I was asking myself ‘Is this what life is all about?’; ‘Is this what I should be doing?’, and I suddenly realized that this is not what I wanted”.

3.4.2 *What Are Alex's Personal Values?*

As discussed in Lichtenstein et al. (2015), pioneering leadership research by Dr Aitken also based on the work of Schwartz (1994) was used to uncover Alex's personal values. At the top of Alex's value system hierarchy is Self-fulfilment which equates to being an Explorer, made up of the values below:

- Meaning of Life (a purpose for living);
- Choosing Own Goals (selecting how to live life);
- Self-Respect (belief in one's own worth)
- A Spiritual Life (emphasis on spiritual, not material matters);
- Mature Love (deep emotional & spiritual intimacy).

The motivational direction & engagement focus based on this value system is motivated by internal and pro-social measures of success and engaged by appealing to personal and others' growth.

The value system of least importance to Alex is Self-approval, including the values of:

- Wealth (material possessions, money)
- Social Power (control over others, dominance)
- Preserving My Public Image (preserving my 'face' and status);
- Authority (the right to lead or command)
- Pleasure (gratification of desires)
- Social Recognition (respect, approval by others)
- Self-Indulgent (Motivated by external and self-centred measures of success).

This is significant as Self-approval and 'winning' is still the dominant values-based discourse in the financial services industry. The 'heads we win, tails you lose' mentality in financial services still dominates. Alex's personal values-based personal-organisational ***misalignment/incongruence*** is obvious.

Alex explained, "We all have to conform to a degree in for example the dress code…I am very individualistic in what I do…if I were asked to do anything at a personal level that made me uncomfortable in terms of conforming, I would either not do it or otherwise I would leave." While Alex pointed out that he had not directly compromised his personal values, he feels there is now a closer alignment of his personal values and the company he has formed.

Of course, Alex could have given a lump sum to a charity if he wanted to feel better or give back and then have a long vacation, but he is working on a new venture, creating jobs and helping people in the long-term. Alex also mentors several start-up micro finance enterprises; he likes sharing some of the skills and knowledge he has built up over the last 30 years.

Alex's case highlights the importance of personal values alignment, also known as Person-Organisation (P-O) fit in the literature. We suggest that for a period of time, an individual may be prepared to suspend his or her personal values in the hopes that the organisation's goals or values may change and align more closely with their personal values. If over time this does not occur, the individual has a choice to make. For example, they may turn a blind eye, speak out, or decide to leave the organisation.

Personal-organisation alignment or congruence is linked to commitment, retention rates, work satisfaction, work attitudes, pro-social behaviour and work performance (e.g., McDonald & Gandz, 1991; Posner et al., 1985). However, what this case illustrates is that ***actual*** values-based congruence and ***apparent*** personal-organisational values-based congruence are neither the same thing, nor permanent (Hewlin, 2009). Hewlin (2003, 2009) describes the phenomenon of an employee suppressing his/her personal values in conjunction with the pretence of expressing values that one does not hold as 'Facades of Conformity'. Employees are capable of masking their true personal values, e.g. ***meaning in life***, and falsely display values they perceive to be organisationally desirable to 'get on'. Whilst this may not be an issue for those who espouse 'Conformity' value system who strive to 'fit in', for employees who strongly espousing Self Direction-oriented motives for action facades of conformity will be linked to psychological discomfort that may well lead to that employee leaving as Alex's case exemplifies (Hewlin, 2009). The psychological distress caused by personal values-based incongruence and 'faking it', sometimes misidentified as 'burnout', should not be underestimated (Hewlin, 2003; Stormer & Devine, 2008).

Questions

Having reviewed Alex's mini case, these questions below may help you to reflect upon your own context:

1. How does the organisational structure and/or culture encourage or inhibit managers in leadership positions to share their personal values?
2. How can I adapt my approach to decision-making and resource allocation, while holding on to my treasured values, and meet a variety of stakeholder needs?
3. How can I learn to confront and navigate with others the moral dilemmas that can occur with the diversity of personal values that exists in my organisation?

We now turn to a case that explores and illustrates values-based team alignment in action.

3.5 Mini-case: Values-Based Team Alignment in Action

Much of the work in and with organisations are in teams making values-based team alignment an essential topic of values-based alignment. Following a brief introduction into the leadership values alignment, this section focuses on the mini case of the sporting legend Phil Jackson, nine-time NBA championship title-winning coach with both the Chicago Bulls (1991–1993, 1996–1998) and the Los Angeles Lakers (2000–2002) which illustrates values-based team alignment in action.

Revisiting the Stakeholder value chain model introduced in the previous chapter, this section focuses on personal values-led team alignment as Reality 1.1—the lynchpin of aligning Reality 1.0 with 2.0. As leadership author Bean (1993, p. 95) explains, "Every enterprise is driven by its leaders' individual and collective values, whether those values are understood or unconsciously influential, spoken or unspoken, written or unrecorded." We can define the leadership team values as the amalgam of motives and personal values of the leadership team, which they role model through their actions and communications. To unpack this even further, see Fig. 3.3 below that illustrates the main components of the values dynamic of leadership teams that strategy is situated in.

Rather than the narrative in the literature of culture 'trumping' strategy or vis-a-versa, it is more helpful to understand the values dynamic as the context that strategising and execution takes place within.

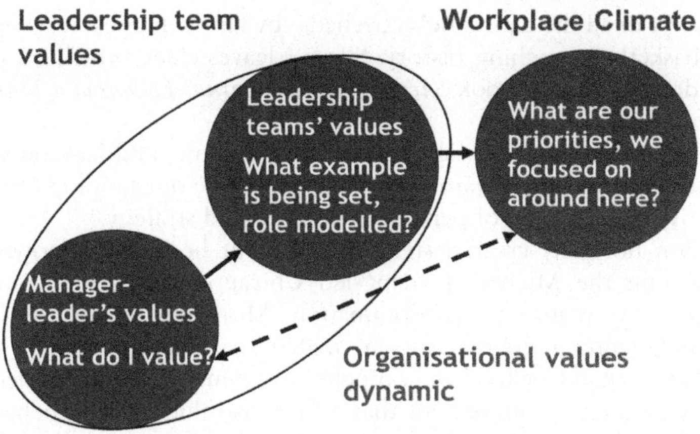

Fig. 3.3 Leadership values dynamic (*Source* Adapted from Concordia International Ltd. [2006])

Unfortunately, our general experience of strategic leadership indicates that knowledge-based cognition is the priority, rather than deep reflection on personal values and their often unconscious impact (Aitken, 2008). Devoid of such personal insight, the espoused language of strategy and business may change without actually changing any intentions, decisions, or actions, of leaders or followers. Personal values allow a deeper dialogue about where the team comes together and pulls apart in a context that provides insight into what's guiding emotions and behaviour (values).

3.5.1 *Mini Case: Taking the Bull by the Horns*

The strategy-as-personal values alignment perspective proposes that strategy should be concerned with creatively shaping the future, not merely trying to predict it. Having a compelling future both personally and organisationally underpinned by intention is a critical success factor. To illustrate the social influencing process that exists between strategists and key stakeholders that impacts upon the emotion (hearts), sense-make/give (minds) and discretionary performance (hands), we've profiled Phil Jackson nine-time NBA championship title-winning coach who has a coaching lifetime winning percentage of 0.725 meaning he's won 72.5% of all the games he's coached—by far the highest in US professional basketball coaching history. Success leaves clues, which we outline below drawn from his book *Sacred Hoops: Spiritual Lessons of a Hardwood Warrior*.

As the most successful basketball coach of all time, Phil Jackson's ability to create a values-based team alignment to achieve outstanding results are instructive for students of personal values-guided strategy.

Jackson not only created stellar results, but he is also renowned for transforming the Michael Jordan[2]-led Chicago Bulls from a one-man show to a five-man team of domination. Moulding a group of macho multi-millionaires with the egos to match that was dominated by one man with a legendary level of competitiveness into a values-aligned team is an extraordinary achievement that makes his values-guided behavioural approach especially appropriate for this pivot. As you are reading the case below you will no doubt be reflecting on what you've created in your life or business and your values-guided strategy.

3.5.2 The Values-Led Vision for the Team

The first thing Phil Jackson did after being named head coach of the Chicago Bulls was to formulate a vision for the team. As he explained, "I had learned from the Lakota (Indians) and my own experience as a coach that vision is the source of leadership, the expansive dream state where everything begins and all is possible. I started by creating a vivid picture in my mind of what the dream could become" (Jackson, 2012, p. 98).

He had a clear intention for the type of team he wanted to create, "I wanted to create a team in which selflessness – not the me-first mentality that had come to dominate professional basketball - was the primary driving force. My goal was to find a structure that would empower *everybody* (author's italics) on the team, not just the stars, and allow the players to grow as individuals as they surrendered themselves to the group effort" (Jackson, 2012, p. 63).

His idea was to use ten players regularly and give the others enough playing time so they could blend in effortlessly with everybody else when

[2] Michael Jordan is universally regarded as the greatest basketball player of all time. In 1999, he was named the greatest North American athlete of the twentieth century by the American cable television sports network ESPN, and he was second to Babe Ruth on the American news agency Associated Press's list of athletes of the century.

they were on the basketball court. This was controversial considering they were a team dominated by one man with a legendary level of competitiveness—Michael Jordan—but it was a calculation that the cohesion it created would be worth the gamble. Jackson explained how his idea paid off in a championship final, "In Game 6 of the 1992 finals against the Portland Trail Blazers, we were down by 17 points in the third quarter and sinking fast. So, I put in the second unit. The rest of the coaching staff, not to mention members of the press, thought I'd finally gone over the edge, but within minutes the subs wiped out the deficit and put us back in the game" (Jackson, 2012, p. 99).

Jackson knew, however, as great as his vision for the team may be that it is never the sole property of one person. So, to make the vision become a reality, it must be owned by every member of the group. Were there obstacles? You bet.

One of the biggest obstacles Jackson had to overcome was the players' dependency on Michael Jordan. So how did he overcome this obstacle and get intellectual and emotional buy-in from the team? Jackson recalls, "(An) important step I took to consolidate the team was to name (Bill) Cartwright co-captain (with Michael Jordan). Naming Cartwright co-captain made the team less Jordan centric…Cartwright knew exactly what I was trying to do, sometimes even better than I did, and could explain it to the younger players in a non-threatening way. He helped me turn them into dreamers, to expand their vision of what they could become" (Jackson, 2012, p. 105).

The other obstacle he had to overcome was getting the players to think more for themselves, what he termed 'thinking power'. He was convinced that for his vision to work, the players would need the confidence to make decisions on their own which couldn't happen if they were constantly searching for directions from the coach. The former coach, Doug Collins, had kept the players and particularly the younger players on a tight rein, frequently yelling at them when they made mistakes. Throughout the game they'd look over at the bench, trying to read Coach Collin's mind. Jackson's approach was the opposite, when they started looking over to him, he cut them off by responding, "What are you looking at me for"? Jackson explained somewhat counter-intuitively, "I wanted them to *disconnect* (original author's italics) themselves from me so they could connect with their teammates – and the game" (Jackson, 2012, p. 105).

How did he get the star Michael Jordan's buy-in? Jordan could see the benefits of the system which transcended what he could achieve on his own. As Jordan explained, "With the talent and *thinking power* (original authors' italics) we had, we were able to open up the court and let one or two guys penetrate, then feed off of them. In the fourth quarter your leadership, your unity, your understanding of the personnel, your fulfilment of roles - all those things come out. And I think that's the way we won" (Jackson, 2012, p. 103).

Coach Jackson led with compassion instead of by fear as the previous coach had done, creating an example to put the 'me' in the service of the 'we' and encouraged his talent to:

- Act with a clear mind—not thinking, just doing,
- Respect the enemy and be aggressive without anger or violence, and.
- Live in the moment and stay calmly focused in the midst of chaos.

> Working with the Bulls I've learned that the most effective way to forge a winning team is to call on the players' need to connect with something larger than themselves...creating a successful team – whether an NBA champion or a record setting sales force - is essentially a spiritual act. It requires the individual to surrender their self-interest for the greater good so that the whole adds up to the sum of its parts. (Jackson, 2012, p. 5)

> More than anything else, what allowed the Bulls to sustain a high level of excellence was the players' compassion for each other's. Love is the force that ignites the spirit and binds the team together. (Jackson, 2012, p. 52)

> He (Michael Jordan) understood that it wasn't brilliant individual performances that made great teams, but the energy that's unleashed when players put their egos aside and work towards a common goal. (Jackson, 2012, p. 21)

Questions

Having read the mini case 'Taking the Bull by the Horns' below are some questions to help you and reflect on it and how it applies to Fig. 3.3 Leadership values dynamic:

- What did the coach value?
- What were the leadership team values?
- How did the changes Coach Jackson make to role model the 'new way' he sought in the team?

3.6 Summary

In this chapter, developing strategies for values-based personal and team alignment has been discussed. Developing personal values-based strategies as a social influencing process was introduced followed by an assessment tool to discover your personal values, the starting point of a values-guided strategy. Reflection points to craft your own values-guided strategy was offered in the context of strategy as storytelling, to increase the changes of intellectual and emotional buy-in by internal and external stakeholders for your strategy. Finally, personal values congruence in action was illustrated in the mini case of Alex that was then put in the context of values-based team alignment in the Taking the Bulls by the Horn mini-case to highlight real-world issues in getting intellectual and emotional buy-in of the team.

The next chapter develops the insights from devising values-guided strategy by focusing on the components of personal values-guided strategy implementation.

Bibliography

Aitken, P. (2008). *Leadership & Change study guide*. Henley Business School.

Aitken, P., & Higgs, M. (2010). *Developing change leaders*. Routledge.

Argyris, C. (1985). *Strategy, change and defensive routines*. Pitman Publishing.

Barry, D., & Elmes, M. (1997). Strategy retold: Toward a narrative view of strategic discourse. *Academy of Management Review, 22*(2), 429–452.

Bean, W.C. (1993). *Strategic Planning that makes thing happen: Getting from where you are to where you want to be*. Human Resource Development.

Burns, J. M. (2003). *Transforming leadership*. Grove Press.

Callandar, J. (2020). *Business Goal Setting: As part of strategy development, what are the key elements in setting business goals that contribute to employee intellectual buy-in?* (DBA thesis). University of Southampton.

Concordia International Ltd. (2006). *Company Information*.

Downing, S., & Henley Management Coll.(United Kingdom). Henley Research Centre. (1999). *Strategic stories: A framework to read them and lead them* (Henley Management College Working paper series, HWP (25)).

Gallup. (2020). *State of the Global Workplace*. https://www.gallup.de/183833/state-the-global-workplace.aspx. Accessed 30 April 2020.

Hales, J. (2007). What do managers do? A critical review of the evidence. *Journal of Management Studies, 23*(1), 88–115.

Hambrick, D. C., & Mason, P. A. (1984). Upper echelons: The organization as a reflection of its top managers. *Academy of Management Review, 9*(2), 193–206.
Hewlin, P. (2003). And the award for best actor goes to ...: Facades of conformity in organizational settings. *Academy of Management Review, 28*(4), 633–642. https://doi.org/10.5465/AMR.2003.10899442
Hewlin, P. (2009). Wearing the Cloak: Antecedents and consequences of creating facades of conformity. *Journal of Applied Psychology, 94*(3), 727–741.
Hitlin, S., & Pinkston, K. (2013). Values, attitudes, and ideologies: Explicit and implicit constructs shaping perception and action. In *Handbook of social psychology* (pp. 319–339). Springer.
Hughes, R. L., & Beatty, K. C. (2005). *Becoming a strategic leader*. Wiley.
Jackson, P. (2012). *Sacred hoops: Spiritual lessons of a hardwood warrior*. Hachette Books.
Kay, J. (1995). *Foundations of corporate success: How business strategies add value*. Oxford Paperbacks.
Latting, J. K., & Ramsey, V. J. (2009). *Reframing change: How to deal with workplace dynamics, influence others, and bring people together to initiate positive change*. ABC-CLIO.
Lichtenstein, S. (2001). The value-based approach to strategy. In T. Garrison (Eds.), *Strategy Dynamics*. Henley management College.
Lichtenstein, S., Aitken, P., & Parry, K. W. (2015). *Personal values systems re-construction and their potential link to diverse leadership purposes: From obscurity to efficacy in leadership development*. Paper presented at 7th Developing Leadership Capacity Conference, Henley Business School, University of Reading.
Lichtenstein, S., Watton, E., & Parry, K. (2016). *True colours: why personal values win out over organisational values when we face ethical dilemmas*. ANZAM.
McDonald, P., & Gandz, J. (1991). Identification of values relevant to business research. *Human Resource Management, 30*(2), 217–236.
McKenzie, J., & Aitken, P. (2012). Learning to lead the knowledgeable organization: Developing leadership agility. *Strategic HR Review, 11*(6), 329–334.
Mintzberg, H. (1987). The strategy concept I: Five Ps for strategy. *California Management Review, 30*(1), 11–24.
Nahapiet, J., & Ghoshal, S. (1998). Social capital, intellectual capital, and the organizational advantage. *Academy of Management Review, 23*(2), 242–266.
Parry, K. W. (1998). Grounded theory and social process: A new direction for leadership research. *Leadership Quarterly, 9*(1), 85–105.
Parry, K. W., & Jackson, B. (2016). Promoting responsibility, purpose, and romanticism in business schools. In S. Kempster & B. Carroll (Eds.), *Responsible leadership: Realism and romanticism*. Routledge.
Pascale, R. T. (1990). *Managing on the edge*. Simon and Schuster.

Posner, B. Z., Kouzes, J. M., & Schmidt, W. H. (1985). Shared values make a difference: An empirical test of corporate culture. *Human Resource Management, 24*(3), 293–309.

Prahalad, C. H., & Hamel, G. (1990). The Core competence of the corporation. *Harvard Business Review, 68*(3), 295–336.

Reich, R. B. (1987). Entrepreneurship reconsidered: The team as hero. *Harvard Business Review, 65*, 77–78.

Robinson, E. (2015). *The psychology of change in organisations: Mindsets and the paradox of continuity* (Doctoral dissertation). University of Cambridge.

Schwartz, S. (1992). Universals in the content and structure of values: Theoretical advances and empirical test in 20 countries. In M. P. Zannam (Ed.), *Advances in experimental social psychology* (Vol. 25, pp. 1–65). Academic Press.

Schwartz, S. H. (1994). Are there universal aspects in the structure and contents of human values? *Journal of Social Issues, 50*(4), 19–45.

Schwartz, S. H., & Bilsky, W. (1987). Toward a theory of the universal content and structure of values: Extensions and cross-cultural replications. *Journal of Personality and Social Psychology, 58*(5), 878.

Stormer, F., & Devine, K. (2008). Acting at work: Facades of conformity in academia. *Journal of Management Inquiry, 17*(2), 112–134.

Toolan, M. (2012). *Narrative: A critical linguistic introduction*. Routledge.

Tsirogianni, S., & Gaskell, G. (2011). The role of plurality and context in social values. *Journal for the Theory of Social Behaviour, 41*(4), 441–465.

CHAPTER 4

Implementing Strategy Based on Personal Values

Abstract This chapter explores the key components of implementing a values-guided strategy. Aligning values-based strategies into the operative values of direct reports is introduced in the context of intellectual and emotional buy-in including drivers for achieving buy-in. Research-based results of the alignment process with high and low-performing teams are summarised before a section on internal communication and how they vary by Settlers, Enterprisers and Explorers are explored to power your values-guided implementation. A consideration of the elements of 'walking the values guided talk' is considered to embed change within the workforce. Finally, a mini case study of Cisco's values-based re-organisation highlights strategy implementation in action.

Keyword Implementation · Values-based alignment · The translation process · Internal communications · Walking the talk

Irrespective of how brilliant the strategy is, its success depends on how well it is understood from the boardroom to the last employee involved in its implementation, their willingness, capability and capacity to implement it (Upadhyay et al., 2013). This willingness to implement the strategy we've called emotional buy-in, and it happens when the strategy aligns with the personal values of internal stakeholders who execute it.

S. Lichtenstein and M. Higgs, *Strategy through Personal Values*,
https://doi.org/10.1007/978-3-030-88269-3_4

This chapter will help readers reflect upon how they can align and translate their missions, goals and strategies into the operative values of those who implement them. In doing so, it will enable intellectual and emotional buy-in for personal values-guided strategy execution.

4.1 Translating Desired Ends into the Operative Values of Direct Reports

Got a strategy? Tick. Tactics? Check. But if formal and informal leaders don't know how to lead a culture with a diversity of values, the strategy may well just stay on the page. Engaging and nourishing employees with diverse personal values releases their resourcefulness and discretionary performance for execution so desperately needed in these disruptive times.

In this section we discuss the critical activity of getting intellectual and emotional buy-in, otherwise known as the translation or alignment process. To create tomorrow's company today methods of creating value, visions, strategies and missions need to be translated into the operative values of employees to implement the strategy, as depicted in Fig. 4.1.

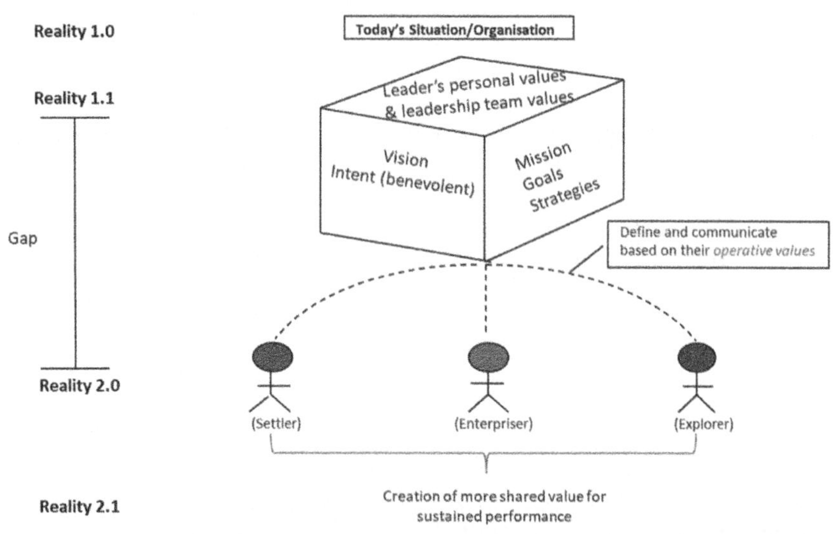

Fig. 4.1 Creating tomorrow's company today (*Source* Adapted from Lichtenstein and Dade [2007])

To create more value for stakeholders, it's imperative to drive our methods for creating value down the organisation. Often this is talked about in abstract terms such as corporate values, but to make them live they need to be translated into the operative values of employees and those implementing the strategy.

Motherhood and apple pie statements like *Respect*, *Integrity*, *Communication* and *Excellence* read like many other organisation's espoused values, and therefore add no competitive advantage. So what good are they other than eyewash for public consumption? Incidentally, the above corporate values were those of disgraced Enron; some guide for action!

As we've said before an organisation's true values as opposed to corporate or core values are the aggregate of personal values, specifically, the dynamic between the CEO's values and those of the employees.

To explore the ways in which we can secure alignment we now turn to the important distinction between different types of values.

4.1.1 Operative vs Adopted Values

Executives' operative values are those dominant personal values that influence 'choice' behaviour as opposed to 'adopted' values—those that are espoused by the organisation. Paarlberg and Perry's (2007) longitudinal study of 52 managers and employees in the public sector concerning the installation of a values alignment system found that strategic values are motivating to employees to the extent that they *reflect employees' operative values*—what they value. Specifically, few employees were able to name the values of the organisation, despite a four-year effort to make all employees aware of the organisations' values! Why? Because there was a disconnect between the content and source of the organisation's 'strategic' values and the employees' operative values (Paarlberg & Perry, 2007).

Feldman (1984) suggests that executives in large organisations deal with tensions between their self-interest and personal values and organisational demands for conformity by developing secret intentions within and between other individuals to protect themselves. By not telling people what they think and value and by not putting one's cards on the table they can't be attacked resulting in a blend of deference behaviour with secrecy: conforming behaviour with secret rejection of the demands for conformity. These conflicts are below the surface as they become undiscussable and ultimately dangerous to the long run health of the organisation because it distorts the truth of what's really going on and emotional buy-in can't be won in these circumstances.

Interviews with employees in the finance industry revealed the conflict between adopted versus operative values led to personal values incongruence (Lichtenstein et al., 2016, p. 10). This is illustrated by an example from an interview with an employee called Pat who valued intellectual autonomy to best serve her clients clashed with the organisation's adopted values of profit-at-all-costs, in her words 'blood sucking ruthlessness', which led to her departure:

> P: 'I was at the [name of organisation] for 3 years. They are very much corporate America, which I don't particularly like … Organisations like [name of company] often don't do what is best for the client, it is based on what gave the biggest fee. So I am now working for an independent, there are 35 of us in the company. Being an independent, means we are not affiliated with anybody. We can say hand on heart we've looked at all the different companies and this is the best one for you, in your situation'.

Voting with one's feet and/or whistle blowing are the ultimate consequences if these distinctions between operative vs adopted values aren't resolved.

With this distinction between operative and adopted values reviewed, the next section looks at key components of the translation process.

4.2 Key Components of the Translation Process: The Seven Drivers of Implementation

This section reviews research-based results concerning the components for successful implementation. Based on a systemic literature review, case studies and interviews with senior practitioners, Schiemann (2009) found seven components for successful alignment including intellectual and emotional buy-in:

1. A clear, agreed-on vision and strategy (Intellectual buy-in)

If top management is not in agreement on the strategy and goals, then alignment throughout the organisation is not possible. Agreeing broad strategic principles but failing to drill down to the level at which real tradeoffs need to be made can hinder alignment.

2. Translation of the vision and strategy into clear, understandable goals and measures—(Intellectual buy-in)

The key challenge is the ability of supervisors to translate and break down the vision, strategy and goals and targets that are meaningful to each individual at different levels of the organisation (Pulakos, 2004; Schiemann, 2009).

3. Acceptance of and passion for the vision, strategy, goals among those who are implementing them (intellectual and emotional buy-in).

According to Ventana Research (Smith, 2008), only about half (52%) of companies do a good job of aligning departmental plans with overarching corporate goals. The key challenge is the ability of supervisors to translate and break down overall strategic objectives into goals and targets that are meaningful to everyone.

4. Clarity regarding individual roles and requirements in supporting the strategic goals—and the extent to which these have been effectively cascaded and interlinked across the organisation—(intellectual buy-in).

Research has found that the most effective practice is to establish a hierarchy of goals where each level supports goals directly relevant to the next level, ultimately working towards the organisation's strategic direction and critical priorities (Pulakos, 2004).

5. Sufficient capabilities (talent, information) and resources to deliver the behaviors needed to reach the goals.

Translating and breaking down the 'new way' capabilities, resources and skills development that are required to support individuals at different levels of the organisation is critical (Argyris, 1985).

6. Clear, timely feedback on goal attainment and the drivers of those goals.

Research has shown that those who receive more frequent and specific performance feedback and coaching are better performers than those who do not (Locke & Latham, 1990; London, 2002). These researchers have shown that feedback that is closer to the performance itself is most effective. This indicates that one-to-one communication with effective coaching skills is a key skill in the process of alignment.

7. Meaningful incentives to encourage employees to develop or deploy sufficient capabilities to achieve the goals.

Whilst research on reward is vast and often contradictory, Schliemann's (2009) meta-analysis found holistic reward systems that reward the collective accomplishments of groups of employees more effective than individual incentive and rewards systems (Gibson, 1995; Schiemann, 2009). Concerning individual reward, it found organisations that can offer more flexible, tailored-to-the-individual reward packages were more likely to reap the benefits of the reinforcing effect of rewards on performance. Based on longitudinal employee survey results, recognition is often rated as important to employees, but appears to be underutilised in many organisations (Schiemann, 2009).

Having summarised key components of alignment, the next section looks at the process of personal values.

4.3 The Social Process of Personal Values Alignment

Paarlberg and Perry (2007) carried out a longitudinal study into the process of translating or aligning employee values with organisational goals. They identified empowering and disempowering practices in the translation process between high and low performing teams in the US Department of Defence. The context was a new system being implemented to align employees to strategic business goals as well as a new HR management system to tie individual performance to the new strategic goals (Paarlberg & Perry, 2007, p. 392). The project gave middle managers increased responsibility to develop individual performance expectations that was designed to communicate the new 'strategic values' to employees as well as to create an understanding and expectation of how individual's performance contributed to organisational performance. Top managers formulated organisation goals and values, communicated those goals and the values they represented, and designed reward and management systems to reinforce those goals and values. Middle managers acted as a conduit of communication, implemented formal systems and then monitored and rewarded compliance with the organisational values (Paarlberg & Perry, 2007).

Drawing on data from 97 interviews with 52 managers and 45 employees, they further segmented the sample between high and low performing teams in terms of motivation and efficiency. Many of the study's insights are contrasted between the practices in high and low performing teams, summarised in Table 4.1. The differences in high performing work units were that middle managers acted as 'integrators' of translating and personalising the missions and goals into their direct reports' operative values. In contrast, middle managers in low performing work units communicated the organisational goals without translating it into employees' daily work-life and what mattered to them.

Key takeaways of Paarlberg and Perry's (2007, p. 405) in-depth research are summarised below:

> ...Our analysis suggests that organizations cannot influence employee behavior by communicating "the values of the organization," as articulated by top leadership through formal presentations or the distribution of laminated cards.' Rather, employees are motivated by what they perceive as being congruent with their operative values.
>
> The process of aligning values is a *social process* that occurs through routine interactions between employees, managers, and perhaps even customers and other stakeholders. These routine interactions reinforce employees' existing values. (Our emphasis)
>
> Middle managers play key roles in integrating individual values through the interpretation of strategic goals. Management tools, particularly in this case, the performance management system, structure the process, providing a formal opportunity to both articulate values and signify which *employee values* are important to the organization's mission. (Our emphasis)

Having considered components and process of alignment, the next section discusses personal values aligning communication for buy-in and it by varies by values orientation so you can tailor your message to people with values other than your own whilst still holding true to your values.

Table 4.1 Summary of findings of Paarlberg and Perry (2007) study in high versus low performing work units

	Low performing work units	*High performing work units*
Employee values that motivate workplace performance		
Source of values:	Increase business; long-term organisation growth and productivity Organisation	To be the best, pride in my work Self: Family teachings, self-worth
Relationship between individual values and strategic goals		
Managers' perception	Technical instruments; use of generic templates, explicit contract	Management as a social process: HR systems provide an opportunity for social interaction; importance of incorporating broad social principles, e.g. Integrity
Employee perceptions	Little connection between organisational goals and daily responsibilities, e.g. 'don't make sense', 'too far removed from my local responsibility'	Perceived connection between broader organisational mission and work unit and individual contribution
		Performance expectations involved personal goals e.g. pursuing higher education
Process	'This is what I want you to do'	"we went back and forth 'till we agreed."
	Electronic communication Standardized, impersonal system	Face-to-face Social process to facilitate work relationships, particularly between themselves and their reports
	Lack of involvement in the process	Ongoing process: give & take dialogue, personal nature of the expectations

Source Adapted from Paarlberg and Perry's (2007) study

4.4 Personal Values-Guided Communication to Internal Stakeholders: Settlers, Explorers and Enterprisers

In Dale Carnegie's (2017, p. 44) book, 'How to make friends and Influence People' originally written in 1936, he offers an anecdote to illustrate a principle of personal values sensitive communications:

> I often went fishing up in Maine during the summer. Personally, I am very fond of strawberries and cream, but I have found that for some strange reason, fish prefer worms. So when I went fishing, I didn't think about what I wanted. I thought about what they wanted. I didn't bait the hook with strawberries and cream. Rather, I dangled a worm or a grasshopper in front of the fish and said: "Wouldn't you like to have that?"

The same psychology applies to gaining values congruence of strategy implementation. The alignment process is a result of interactions and communication and subsequent 'fit' between the organisation and internal stakeholders' personal values which results in discretionary performance to execute strategy (Chapman, 1991; House et al., 1996; Zhang et al., 2008).

This section offers practical application for values alignment concerning internal communication with the values orientations of Settlers, Enterprisers and Explorers. In this format we can only offer brief rules of thumb, which is based on our own research and that of campaign and communications advisor Rose (2011) based on CDSM's Ltd consumer values-based segmentation. Lichtenstein et al. (2015) conducted a study of 3,015 in-work UK to explore the relationship between in-work employees' personal values and their preferences for organisational outcomes and behaviour. Employees were from the ages of 15–73 across socio-economic classes and industries and the data was subjected to Exploratory and Confirmatory factor analysis to examine 3 propositions:

(i) whether work outcomes and behaviours were structured by the same factor solution that best explained personal value systems (PVS),
(ii) whether PVS and work outcomes and behaviours were second-order latent constructs; in other words, whether the data is best explained by motives for action or the individual items on their own, and finally,
(iii) that personal value system (PVS) would positively impact work behaviours and outcomes.

All three propositions were supported by the analysis. The results of the work outcomes and behaviour provides the basis of a personal values-based employee-alignment diagnostic as well as insights into the different

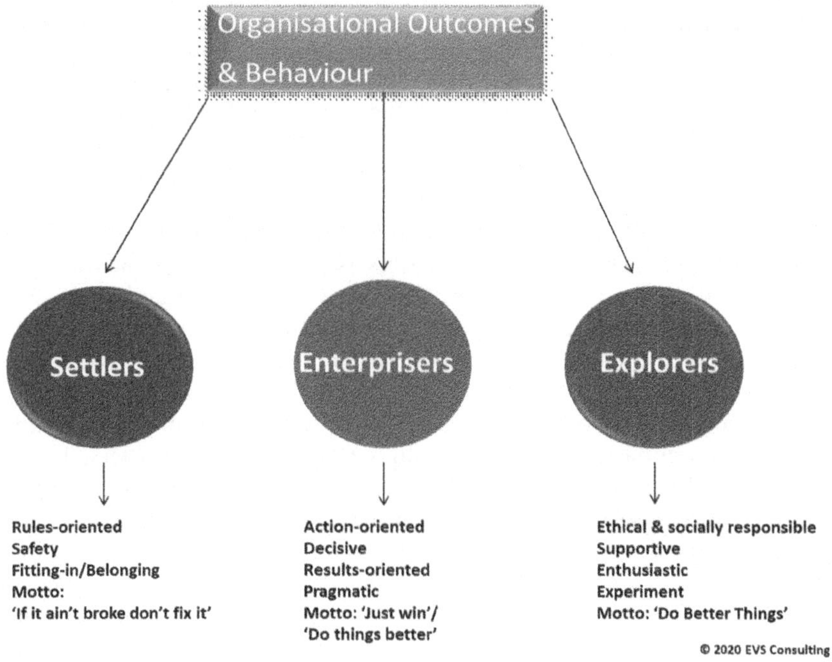

Fig. 4.2 Values orientation types

worlds of Settlers, Enterprisers and Explorers for implementation as seen in Fig. 4.2.

The insights from research and experience are offered below to enhance buy-in for the alignment process of internal stakeholders with different values orientations.

4.4.1 Audience

The first consideration concerning internal communications is the intended audience. Regarding audience, several things to consider are (Rose, 2011):

- Who are you primarily already engaging with: Settlers, Enterprisers or Explorers?,

- Which values orientation are you coming from: personally, as a group or organisation?, and
- Who do you need to engage with, build support for or deepen the relationship with?

Settlers, Enterprisers and Explorers have clear preferences for communication, so the rules of thumb in the tables below can be a useful guide for internal communications preferences by values orientation. There are never absolutes, but these rules of thumb can help in the design of internal communications regarding channels and context below (see Table 4.2).

The messenger, or by whom the initiative comes from, can have a powerful effect. If one was going to have a launch for a strategic initiative, below in Table 4.3 are some rules of thumb regarding internal communication messengers with the highest impact for the three values orientations.

Strategy initiatives and policies include actions to execute them, what you require those who implement to do. Below in Table 4.4 are rules of thumb for action steps by the three values orientations.

These rules of thumb hopefully provide guidance to translating your values-guided methods of creating more value for shareholders into the operative values of Settlers, Enterprisers and Explorers to get them executed farther and faster. By doing so it is hoped your sense-give

Table 4.2 Channels and context by values orientations

Settler	*Enterprisers*	*Explorers*
Face-to-Face Familiar channels of a familiar nature Official channels used by authority Traditional family fun and entertainment	Social media which allows f-2-f Entertainment, venues, special occasions, that are exclusive Competitions Parties, where participants and families can have their 15 minutes of fame	Face-to-Face Cultural venues (e.g. cinema, museums and music events) and organisations that allows for exploration and exchange of ideas Gatherings and events to ponder big issues, e.g. a facilitated group events Nature/outdoors New innovate experiences

Source Adapted from Rose (2011)

Table 4.3 Preferred messenger by values orientations

Settler	*Enterprisers*	*Explorers*
Boss at work—if I feel I belong there, looked after and respected	Those in positions of power	Someone interesting, e.g. a thought leader
Someone they know well—established and known	Well known business leaders/ 'sage on the stage'	Someone authentic (versus famous) who has the reason to know 'the truth'
Traditional or respected figure of authority	High achievers who are famous for being rich or successful	
The leader of a group or 'tribe', e.g. group or union	Anyone famous, e.g. people in gossip magazines	
	Sports personalities	
	TV personalities, e.g. bloggers	

Source Adapted from Rose (2011)

capability will be enhanced by thinking in terms of values orientations. By thinking through how strategies may play with different values orientations will instantly make you the smartest person in the room!

Having offered some rules of thumb for the 'talk' of personal values-guided communication and how it varies by Settlers, Explorers and Enterprisers, the next section considers 'the walk' or signalling the key messages to the workforce.

4.5 Walking the Values-Guided Talk: Signalling

People are experts at detecting whether others' actions are congruent or incongruent with their words. 'Walking the talk' refers to formal and informal leaders' implicitly and explicitly connecting their 'walk' behaviour to their values-guided authentic 'talk' to enable concerted role modelling that offers distinct cues for followers about what is expected of them within their own spheres of influence (Aitken, 2007). Leaders must know the look of their walk and its precise link to the values origin of their talk, before attempting to influence followers (Aitken & Higgs, 2010). This advice follows a long line of authors such as Taylor (2005, p. 351) who appeals to leaders "to make the links specific between what you do and the values and beliefs that underpin this".

Often the priorities and signals to the workforce get lost due to a lack of clarity of what the priority and focus should be. Clear signalling by the formal and informal leadership cascaded throughout the organisation can

Table 4.4 Preferred messages by values orientations

Settler	*Enterprisers*	*Explorers*
Dos		
Stick to the knitting Officially approved Uncomplicated Routine with high certainty, e.g. a standard operating procedure As familiar as possible Risk reducing Enhances safety, security and belonging	Change a stitch Recommended Simple Achievable Visible, displayable Recognised, applauded, esteem-building Rewarded Fun, sociable, stimulating Has an immediate impact Proven, 'best practice' Allow options, and bending the rules	Innovative: create a new type of yarn from high tech material Novel Intriguing Ethical About beauty, nature or justice Complex Surprising Authentic Stimulating About ideas, theories, possibilities About the big picture Allow them to define the problem, what's right & wrong and ask questions Choose from open options
Don'ts		
Create new ways of doing things Be the first to do anything Look at the 'big picture' Explore the unknown	Innovate Anything traditional or old fashion 'just follow the rules' Make them give things up Do things for others with no social reward Just because its ethical, an idea or theory Lead in a debate or controversy Embrace an open-ended problem	Do the conventional or comply with routine Closed options Go on the recommendations of others Because it's bigger or best Because it's always been done this way It's required by authority

Source Adapted from Rose (2011)

amplify what the attention focus and priority should be to the workforce. Based on Argyris (1985), the signals below can be used to send clear cues and expectations to the workforce through congruence between the 'walk' and the values-guided 'talk' in Table 4.5.

As an example of signalling, one of us was delivering a leadership workshop to high-ranking civil servants at the then UK National School of

Table 4.5 Signals for 'walking the talk' congruence

Signal	*Example*
Physical symbols	A new chief executive may choose to turn his/her large office, with the inspiring view, into the staff rest area
Reward and recognition focus	Reinforcement of the newly required values can be done through pay and benefits as well as specific personal acknowledgements
Repeated attention paid to priorities	At every turn, delegation of a task can be explained as connected to a part of the strategy. If 'innovation' is the new rally cry, what number agenda item is it?
Behaviour in crisis situations	An emergency gives leaders the spotlight where a message or response has immediate emotional resonance and is therefore remembered, for good or bad
Time devoted to role modelling the priority	How much personal time and energy does the leadership put aside to demonstrate the culture change priorities he/she has set for others?

Source Based on Argyris (1985)

Government. We were discussing signalling as a leadership skill to manifest personal values-guided strategy implementation, at which point the delegates shared how they were still buzzing from the week's event of the arrival of a new minister for the then Department of Trade and Industry. On the minister's first day on the job, he ate at the canteen and upon finishing his meal, sent a handwritten note to the head cook thanking him for a delicious meal. The story of the minister's note to the head cook spread like wildfire through the whole department. What needs by the receiver, the head cook, were being fulfilled by that note? That's right, significance. How many of our employees have an invisible sign around their chest saying, 'Make me feel important'? All of them. Whether they are working remotely or not. What message do you think the minister's note signalled to the workforce/civil servants? How much did it cost that minister to write that note? We'd want to look for more cues over time by the minister to judge intentions and congruence, however, what a simple yet powerful example of signalling on one's first day!

4.6 Mini Case: Cisco—Re-organising to Collaborate

Having discussed the implementation of values guided strategy, below is a mini-case on Cisco's reorganisation that highlights issues raised in this chapter with questions at the end.

Cisco provides the plumbing for the technology world. A near-death experience during the dot com bust in 2001 led to an epiphany by ex-CEO John Chambers: "This world belongs to those who know how to collaborate" (McGirt, 2008). At Cisco, the focus was on three pillars of collaboration: culture, process and technologies. To transform business and successfully drive results, it was every team's role to revisit business processes, establish a collaborative culture, and then employ appropriate collaborative technology.

4.6.1 From a 'Cowboy Culture' to Collaboration

In reflecting on the dot com bust, Chambers talked of the dark days of 2001 that led to the emergence of the radically different Cisco. In the pre-2001 Cisco, it had a hard-nosed approach to doing business with the bottom 10% in sales each year let go and sales forecasts twice a week. In the company's old 'cowboy culture' days of 2001, strong personalities were rewarded for jostling one another out of the way to get Chambers' approval. "In 2001, we were like most high-tech companies, with one or two primary products that were really important to us," he explains. "All decisions came to the top 10 people in the company, and we drove things back down from there." Tony Bates, who ran the $12.5 billion service-provider group explained, "We had purchased all these companies, we didn't even know what they did," he says. Without the reorganisation, he adds, "we'd still be thinking in a straight line, pure cowboy. It was an important shock to the system."

Chambers took Cisco through a massive, radical, often bumpy reorganisation. The bumpy part was that the leaders of business units formerly competing for power and resources now had to share responsibility for one another's success.

4.6.2 Change from the Top

So, what did the change to collaborative leadership look like? "Instead of looking at how well we're doing, we're asking ourselves what we can do to be better" (McGirt, 2008). The goal was to spread the company's leadership and decision-making to working groups that currently involve 500 executives. This move, Chambers said, reflected a new philosophy about how business can best work in a networked world.

The other goal was to get more products to market faster, and Chambers relished the results. "The boards and councils have been able to innovate with tremendous speed. One week to get a [business] plan that used to take six months!" They moved to a network of councils and boards empowered to launch new businesses, plus an evolving set of Web 2.0 technology—not to mention a new financial incentive system—encourage executives to work together like never before. After he launched the reorganisation into boards and councils, "there were times when everyone, even the CEO, was very uncomfortable," he admits. The internal economy of the old Cisco was very much market based. Chambers chose to redistribute the wealth: Executives compensation was changed to how well the collective of businesses performs, not their own individual product units. Playing well with others was also an increasingly important part of rank-and-file employees' performance reviews. There was a wall of cultural resistance for these changes, Chambers says, and some **20% of his executives left**. "Explaining to people why we needed to change things was the hard part."

Chambers wanted nothing less than a total redesign of the corporation. Starting at the top: "You won't have to depend on the CEO anymore." About those Cisco executives who left, he says he came to realise that "some people need a command-and-control environment." But that's not the way of the future: "We now have a whole pool of talent who can lead these working groups, like mini CEOs and COOs. We're growing ideas, but we're growing people as well." In fact, he says, "where I might have had two potential successors, I now have 500."

Boards and councils were created that are cross-functional, interdepartmental, even international teams of executive 'volunteers,' who organise themselves around major initiatives or specific product lines. As an example: Ron Ricci, who translates Chamber's ideas into action, convened a board of self-identified sports fans to brainstorm how Cisco might tap into the sports business. Without buy-in or even permission from Chambers, they brought in 15 people with relevant skills—turning down an invitation to collaborate is not an option—and built a product called StadiumVision, which allows venue owners to broadcast video and digital content, including targeted advertising, to fans in the stadium. Ultimately, the board collaborated with sales and marketing to win contracts with the Arizona Cardinals and the New York Yankees US baseball teams, and the Dallas Cowboys US football team. A multimillion-dollar business came together in less than 120 days.

4.6.3 Culture, Processes and Technology

"We want a culture where it is unacceptable not to share what you know," Chambers said. So, he promoted all kinds of social networking at Cisco: You could write a blog, upload a video, and tag your myriad strengths in the Facebook-style internal directory. Cisco citizens are blogging, vlogging, and virtualising, using social-networking tools that they've made themselves and that, in many cases, far exceed the capabilities of the commercially available wikis, YouTubes, and Facebooks created up the road in Palo Alto. 'C-Change' is its collaborative business process as part of its 'Integrated Workforce Experience (IWE)', the collaborative tools that Cisco has developed for businesses.

The open-source nature of the culture has yielded results. The team of Mike Mitchell, the director of technology communications, created 'C-Vision' a YouTube inside the firewall that has become one of the company's most popular communication tools. Most of the videos are short product reports, sales ideas and engineering updates, all created deskside and published directly to the network with the click of a mouse. No filter, no lawyers.

Across the company, Ricci says, fiscal 2008 saw "a tenfold increase in new projects." And he points out that operating expenses have been trimmed from about 38% at the height of the tech boom to between 35 and 36% following the re-organisation: "We're [adding] 2% to 3% of profit off of every dollar of revenue we get in."

4.6.4 The Role of the CEO

Ricci admits, "I think that culture is really a reflection of the CEO personality. It's possible Larry Ellison (Executive chairman of Oracle Corp.) would make a great CEO of Cisco, in terms of his business skill, but he's so different from John that he would probably spend the next 20 years trying to make the company be like him." Ricci believes that Cisco's guideline for collaboration is a great way to run a company and build a great workforce, "but only if it is what the CEO believes that this is how people should behave." Because if top executives have to cede control over their resources, the CEO does too. At Cisco, Chambers says, the ratio of distributed innovation to traditional decision-making is about 70–30. "That's the right mix for us." But the ratio is not set in stone. Unlike last-century manufacturing-based leadership systems like Six Sigma that are designed to make management consistent and predictable, Ricci says, "we want to add variability, not remove it." So, companies have to find the right mix for them.

Questions

- How do you think Chambers own values help or hinder the collaboration culture he sought to create?
- What were the new leadership team values Chambers sought?
- How did Chambers signal and role model the 'new way' strategic leadership team values away from the "cowboy culture" and "command-and-control environment"? Why did 20% of his team leave?
- In what ways was the workplace climate focused on the new way?

4.7 Summary

In this chapter, implementing values-based strategies has been discussed. The translation process was introduced in the context of operative vs adopted values, before considering the drivers of strategy implementation including emotional and intellectual buy-in. Next, results from low and high performing teams from research into the social influencing alignment process was reviewed. Personal values-based inter-personal influencing strategies for Settlers, Enterprisers and Explorers were summarised followed by a summary of 'walking the talk' and workforce implementation. Finally, the mini case of Cisco underscores concepts of values-guided strategic change introduced in this section.

Bibliography

Aitken, P. (2007). 'Walking the talk': The nature and role of leadership culture within organisation culture/s. *Journal of General Management, 32*(4), 17–37.

Aitken, P., & Higgs, M. (2010). *Developing change leaders*. Routledge.

Argyris, C. (1985). *Strategy, change and defensive routines*. Pitman Publishing.

Brandel, J., Zepeda, M., Scholtz, A., & Williams, A. (2020, July 30). *Pivot to People: It's Time to Build the New Economy*. https://medium.com/zebras-unite/pivot-to-people-its-time-to-build-the-new-economy-75a624eaf38a. Accessed 16 March 2021.

Carnegie, D. (2017). *How to win friends & influence people*. e-artnow.

Carrington, D. (2019, October, 13). Firms ignoring climate crisis will go bankrupt, says Mark Carney. *Guardian*.

Chapman, J. A. (1991). Matching people and organisations: Selection and socialization in public according firms. *Administrative Science Quarterly, 36*, 459–484.

Collis, D. J., & Rukstad, M. G. (2008). Can you say what your strategy is? *Harvard Business Review, 86*(4), 82–90.

Ecological Footprint. (2021). https://www.footprintnetwork.org/our-work/ecological-footprint/. Accessed 13 July 2021.

Feldman, D. C. (1984). The development and enforcement of group norms. *Academy of Management Review, 9*(1), 47–53.

Gibson, V. M. (1995, February). The new employee reward system. *Management Review*, 13–18.

House, R. J., Shane, S. A., & Herold, D. M. (1996). Rumors of the death of dispositional research are vastly exaggerated. *Academy of Management Review, 21*(1), 203–224.

Lichtenstein, S., & Dade, P. (2007). The shareholder value chain: Values, vision and shareholder value creation. *Journal of General Management, 33*(1), 15–31.

Lichtenstein, S., Higgs, M., & Samuel, P. (2015). *Can employee values predict work behaviour?* British Academy of Management.

Lichtenstein, S., Watton, E., & Parry, K. (2016). *True colours: why personal values win out over organisational values when we face ethical dilemmas*. ANZAM.

Locke, E. A., & Latham, G. P. (1990). *A theory of goal setting and task performance*. Prentice-Hall.

London, M. (2002). *Job feedback* (2nd ed.). Lawrence Erlbaum Associates.

Lorsch, J., Lorsch, J. W., & Tierney, T. J. (2002). *Aligning the stars: How to succeed when professionals drive results*. Harvard Business Press.

Mackie, D., & Murray, J. (2020, January 14). *Risky business: The climate and the macroeconomy*. Economic Research, J.P. Morgan Securities.

McGirt, E. (2008, November 25). *How Cisco's CEO John Chambers is turning the Tech Giant Socialist*. FastCompany.

Paarlberg, L. E., & Perry, J. L. (2007). Values management: Aligning employee values and organization goals. *The American Review of Public Administration, 37*(4), 387–408. *Harvard Business Review, 70*(1), 71–79

Pulakos, E. D. (2004). *Performance management*. SHRM Foundation. Effective Practices Guidelines.

Rose, C. (2011). *What Makes People Tick: The three hidden worlds of settlers, prospectors and pioneers*. Matador.

Rushe, D. (2021, March 30, Tuesday). Green investing 'is definitely not going to work', says ex-BlackRock executive. *The Guardian*. https://www.theguardian.com/business/2021/mar/30/tariq-fancy-environmentally-friendly-green-investing?CMP=Share_iOSApp_Other. Accessed 30 March 2021.

Schiemann, W. A. (2009). Aligning performance management with organizational strategy, values, and goals. In J. W. Smither & M. London (Eds.), *Performance management: Putting research into action* (pp. 45–87). Wiley.

Smith, M. (2008). Sales and operations planning: Making BPM work. *Business Performance Management, 6*(1), 4–8.

Taylor, C. (2005). *Walking the talk—Building a culture for success*. Random House.

Upadhyay, A. Y. A., Upadhyay, A. K., & Palo, S. (2013). Strategy implementation using balanced scorecard: Achieving success through personal values of leaders and employees. *Management and Labour Studies, 38*(4), 447–469.

Zhang, X., Austin, S., Glass, J., & Mills, G. (2008). Toward collective organizational values: A case study in UK construction. *Construction Management and Economics, 26*(10), 1009–1028.

CHAPTER 5

Postscript: Where Are We Now and Emerging Trends in Personal Values Guided Strategy

Abstract This chapter explores where personal values-guided strategy has been, where it is now and emerging trends in the field. Firstly, the subject as an academic discipline is mapped onto the issue lifecycle in a historical management context to assess where it is now. Next, emerging trends in personal values-guided adaptive strategies is discussed in the context of values-aligned generative business models. Finally, emerging links with moral orientations with practical application to stakeholder governance is illustrated by ex-Unilever CEO Paul Polman's personal values-led Sustainable Living strategy.

Keyword Extractive and generative business models · Moral orientation · Corporate governance

It's a curiosity of personal values-guided strategy that although it's been around since the 1960s, it is still in its early stages of development. Personal values have been absolutely central to strategy since the inclusion of the personal values of senior management as one of the four driving forces behind the formulation and implementation of corporate strategy in the Harvard Policy Model in the 1970s (Andrews, 1980; Freeman et al., 1988). And yet, we are only just beginning to understand the implications of the unconscious power of personal values at work.

S. Lichtenstein and M. Higgs, *Strategy through Personal Values*, https://doi.org/10.1007/978-3-030-88269-3_5

This chapter will help contextualise the field and highlight emerging themes.

5.1 Values-Based Strategy in the Issue Lifecycle

Let's face it, management is a fad industry. As such, values-based strategy as an academic subject has ridden the peaks and troughs of the management issue lifecycle with its familiar phases of development, early growth, shakeout, maturity/establishment and decline. Guth and Taguri's (1965) seminal Harvard Business Review article 'Personal values and corporate strategy', marked the first phase of its development. The role of personal values and strategy grew and reached establishment with its inclusion in the Harvard Policy Model in the 1970s but went into decline in the 'greed is good'/'lunch is for wimps' go-go 1980s. A resurgence of values in strategy took place with Peter's and Waterman's (1982). In Search of Excellence that spawned the ubiquitous McKenseys 7's model, which identified shared values as a 'soft' factor of organisational effectiveness. This was bolstered by Hambrick and Mason's (1984) and Finkelstein and Hambrick's (1998) ground-breaking works that launched Strategic Leadership as a field, which proposed executives' personal values are reflected in their strategic choices. However, the field slipped into shakeout and was eclipsed by the deterministic, analytical Planning school of Strategy identified with Michael Porter's work (Mintzberg, 2003). Barrett's (1998) 'Liberating the Corporate Soul' generated some interest amongst practitioners as well as consulting, but it's complexity and focus on corporate culture has arguably limited its applicability to personal values-guided strategy.

Its continued niche appeal has largely part been self-inflicted: strategists had neither the tools nor the access to managers willing to have their personal values poked and prodded. Instead, researchers sought publications using demographic variables such as age, social class, tenure and levels of education as proxies for more fundamental characteristics of executive judgements such as personal values. Although the use of demographics as proxies has been severely criticised, it's expediency made it far easier to research and get published. Moreover, confusion between work values, corporate values, core values, organisational values, employee values and other types of values has also limited the field's coherence and consistency as a topic. In light of all these other types of values, personal values-guided strategy has no doubt suffered from the 'jingle fallacy'—the phenomenon of conflating constructs which superficially appear and sound similar, but are fundamentally distinct (Kelley, 1927).

Powell et al.'s (2011, p. 1377) clarion call re-casting the strategic leadership school of strategy to 'Behavioural Strategy' has breathed new life into personal values-guided strategy: "The strategic context of strategic management involves organizationally situated managers, widespread uncertainty, and poorly defined problems with unknowable social and economic consequences. In th (ese) circumstances, we believe strategy research should increase its emphasis on executive judgement in the actual conditions of high-stakes, complex problem solving in organizations". Personal values-guided strategy is but a minute sub-set of the vast Behavioural Strategy field, however, all boats rise in the tide of its growth in scholarship and interest.

To be clear, we distinguish between personal values-guided strategy and personal values research, the latter being vast and continually growing. Personal values research is largely divorced from examining personal values in the context of managerial judgement in the workplace. Instead personal values research is inter-disciplinary and vast, focusing on educational contexts, as an explanatory value of attitudes or as a moderating variable in inter-generational studies, such as Millennial's attitudes or attitudes to 'green issues' like Corporate Social Responsibility (CSR). When personal values research does involve a business context it tends to be based on research with first-year undergraduate students, which again is disconnected from the real world of work.

So where are we now? Personal values-guided strategy falls into the 'cognitive school' of strategy that views strategy as a mental process (Mintzberg et al., 1998). As such, Mintzberg et al.'s (1998, p. 172) damning critique of this school in 1998 is still accurate today, "This school is characterised more by it's potential than by its contributions. The central idea is valid...but strategic management has yet to gain sufficiently from cognitive psychology. Or, perhaps more accurately, cognitive psychology has yet to address adequately the questions of prime interest to strategic management." So in brief, the state of personal values-guided strategy is 'not good enough'. But there are reasons for its renewed growth that can be found in emerging trends in the field.

5.2 Emerging Trends: Transformational Adaptive Strategies

Regardless of the academic issue lifecycle, Strategy as personal values congruence has the promise of moving into early growth again because it has struck the zeitgeist. There is a palpable thirst for an alternative to the short-term bottom-line way of doing business, which is reflected in movements such as 'Responsible leadership', 'ethical leadership', 'Conscious capitalism' and other such romantic notions, which have largely withered in the face of bare-fisted capitalism. One of the really exciting developments in personal values-guided strategy are personal values aligned transformational strategies that are challenging the status quo and likely to be here to stay.

Much like the Great Financial Crash (GFC) of 2008 that laid bare self-serving agendas of the 'banksters' and a failure of corporate governance that sowed the seeds of the Occupy Wall St protests of 2011, the Covid-19 pandemic has exposed similar fissures and dysfunctionalities in 'business as usual'. This is currently referred to as the 'K' recovery: where the upper path of the K are the 'have mores' that are able to work remotely, and the lower path are the front-line 'have nots'. Urgency has been added to the debate due to ecocide—mass damage and destruction of ecosystems—highlighted by the much-publicised IPPC reports declaring man-made climate damage is irreversible and we have until 2030 to act to avoid catastrophic consequences (IPPC, 2021).

In late stage Capitalism in the Global North that resembles the end of a game of Monopoly, we are faced with economies that can't economise, welfare systems in which the poor don't fare well, police that can't enforce the law or brutalise segments they are supposed to protect and serve, judicial systems without justice and schools that can't teach. In the midst of another epidemic, one of joined-up, long-term strategy with benevolent intent, at the deepest level we are having to ask ourselves, what does success look like in a system that is failing the many?

The World Economic Forum's (2020) Global Risks Reports declared that the renewing and improving the architecture of our national and international political and **economic** systems is this generation's defining task. Brandel et al. (2020, p. 2) writes, "The most significant and transformative human rights project is one that has received little attention within the human rights domain: challenging the corporation itself and reimagining our economic enterprises. Allow us to paraphrase: The most urgent human rights project of our time is reimagining business."

The next section reviews strategies of adoption to the changing business landscape.

5.2.1 *Values-Based Transformational Strategies*

As discussed in Chapter 1, today's humanity is using the equivalent of 1.6 Earths to provide the resources we use and absorb our waste (Ecological Footprint, 2021). Based on Raworth's (2021) Doughnut Report, as seen in Fig. 5.1 we are overshooting the planetary boundaries of climate change, ocean acidification, chemical pollution, nitrogen & phosphorus

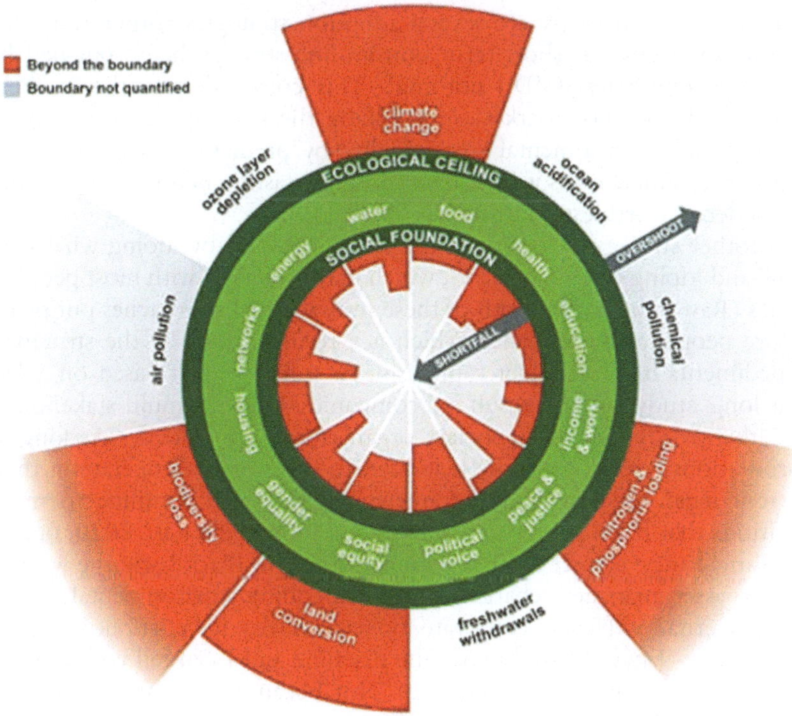

Fig. 5.1 Doughnut Transgressions (*Source* Doughnut Report [2020])

loading, freshwater withdrawals, land conversion, biodiversity loss, air pollution and ozone layer depletion whilst undershooting human needs as defined by the United Nation's Sustainability Development Goals agreed by 193 member countries in 2015 to be achieved by 2030 (UN, 2015) in Annex.

These disruptions and others to come such as AI and robotics, future pandemics and other social, political and economic risks provoke strategic responses by business. The impact of the continued 'Anthropocene Extinction', the first extinction event in the history of the planet to be caused by one species—humans (Barnosky et al., 2012) has been analysed in Mackie and Murray's (2020) recent report for J. P. Morgan (n.d.) entitled 'Risky Business: The Climate and the Macroeconomy', which details the catastrophic impact of climate change on human longevity, immigration and conflicts.

In this context, there are several adoption strategies corporations can pursue. One obvious short-term bottom-line strategy being pursued by extractive industries is 'Do nothing'. This comes despite the ex-Bank of England governor Mark Carney linking the two aspects of economic viability and environmental sustainability by predicting that firms' that ignore the climate crisis will go bankrupt, forecasting pension funds could be rendered worthless (Carrington, 2019).

Another strategy is to reform the current system by 'doing what pays now' and 'doing one's fair share', which may well align with most people's values (Raworth, 2021). Both of these transactional approaches put profit before people and the planet, which is a result in part by the structural impediments of shareholder capitalism. As a final report based on a 10-year-long study on the result of companies forming multi-stakeholder initiative (MSIs) with civil society organisations concluded, "As long as corporations remain primarily beholden to investors and operate in their current legal and governance frameworks, they will continue to make decisions that harm people and the planet." (Brandel et al., 2020, pp. 3–4). Tariq Fancy, former chief investment officer at BlackRock, the world's largest asset manager, charged with embedding environmental, social and governance (ESG) corporate policies across its portfolio recently concluded, "I have looked inside the machine and I can tell you business does not have this (climate change). Not because these are bad people but because they run for-profit machines that will operate exactly as you would expect them to do…It's not because they are evil, it's because the system is built to extract profits" (Rushe, 2021). The added risk of the 'doing one's fair share' approach is that it may well descend into a race-to-the-bottom of 'I'll do my share when 'x' does there's'.

Finally, the third values-based adoption strategy is transformation, which requires a deep reflection of purpose and system: a local, ecological and social impact-minded re-visioning of wealth and society that includes a structural shifting of power. This will align with still fewer people's values.

Underpinning this dialogue concerning the architecture of business are personal values-guided strategic preferences which are outlined in the next section.

5.3 Values-Guided Strategies Revisited: Explorers, Enterprisers and Settlers

In the previous chapters we've outlined the different worlds of Settlers Enterprisers and Explorers. Underlying needs and values orientations are reflected in predictable patterns of strategy preferences as outlined in Table 5.1 and applied to the adaptive strategies of incrementalism, reform and transformation.

In applying values-based strategy preferences to adaptive strategies, it's worth noting that in the dynamics of change, Explorers create the innovations that are then adopted by Explorers and ultimately Settlers. For example, policies developed by the Explorers such as development breaks/sabbaticals that are accepted as normal today would have been

Table 5.1 Proposed methods of creating shareholder value by executive values orientation

	Settler	Enterpriser	Explorer
Motto	If it ain't broke don't fix it	Be a winner	Make it novel
Vision	Tried and tested	Best practice	Innovation
Goal	Safe haven	Do things better	Do better things
Market Strategy	Protect and defend market	2nd-but-better	1st-to-market innovator
Adaptive strategy	Incrementalism	Reform	Transformation

Source Adapted by Lichtenstein and Dade (2007)

seen as radical or unnecessary 50 years ago. From Levi's jeans worn by the 'hippies' that are now commonplace with septuagenarian Settlers to Fairtrade coffee first developed by Café' Direct and now common-place amongst status quo coffee companies, this similar diffusion of ideas and innovation persists.

Building on last section's categorisation of adaptive corporate strategies to the undershoot of human needs and the overshoot of the planet's ecological boundaries, we categorise the adaptive strategies to the current and future challenges and disruptions to business as *transformational*, *incremental* and *reform*. We now put this in a values-guided context. Our proposition is that increasingly we will see personal values-based transformational strategies from the Explorers whilst Enterprisers and Settlers will continue to pursue incrementalistic and reformist strategies, respectively. Below the values-guided adaptive strategies are discussed.

5.3.1 Explorer Type Transformational Strategy: Extractive vs Generative Values-Based Strategies

Businesses like Interface, a business in the carpet manufacturing industry, is transitioning from an extractive 'take-make-use-and lose' business model illustrated on the left in Fig. 5.1 to an Explorer-type 'Mission Zero' transformational strategy based on a regenerative business model that seeks to restore and regenerate the Earth's resources as seen on the right in Fig. 5.2.

In the context of 1.6 Earth's resources being depleted every year and 68% loss of biodiversity of animals, plants, birds, fish, insects, and forests in the last 50 years, sustainability is no longer an option: one cannot be sustainable with a devastated habitat (Ecological Footprint, 2021; WWF, 2020). Therefore, the trend will be for Explorers to pursue regenerative models that are holistic where the conditions for life in all its guises are enhanced upon, which includes re-vitalising, renewing, and regenerating both community and planet for the survival of our communities and all other species including our own (Ubiquity University, 2021).

What is novel in this new Zeitgeist is that companies aren't just retrofitting extractive models onto existing ones but are starting with generative models *by design* that align with leadership's values and increasingly youth leadership. This encompasses a nested design of ownership, governance, purpose, finance and networks *by design*. These values-guided

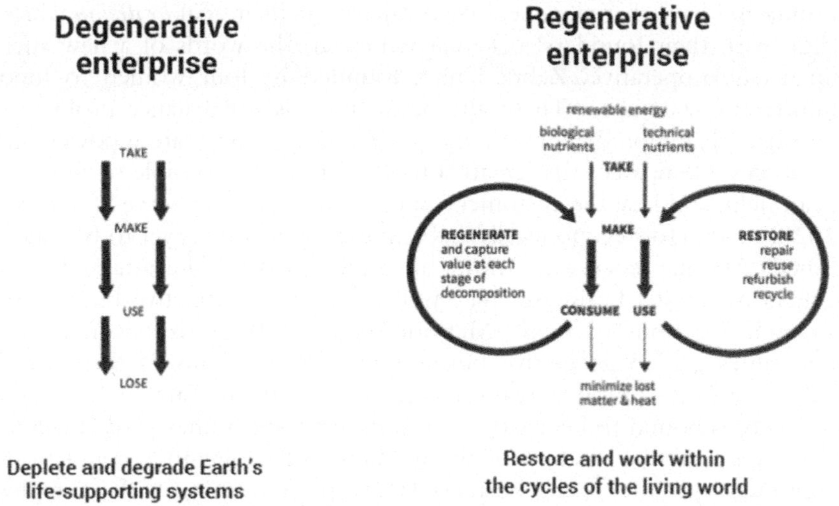

Fig. 5.2 Extractive vs Regenerative business models (*Source* Raworth [2021])

strategies include alternative forms of ownership structure which are superior at distributing the benefits of the business to its stakeholders.

5.3.1.1 Alternative Generative Models

Alternative organisational forms to the PLC model are nothing new and include co-operatives, B corps, kinship systems, groups, networks, communes, tribes, partnerships, local exchange trading systems, trusts, Community Land Trusts, foundations, NGOs, clubs, Employee-owned co-operatives, societies, foundations, associations, charities, non-profits, villages, credit unions, and hybrids of all the above such as supporter-owned football clubs like Bayern Munich and Barcelona and the Green Bay Packers of the US National Football League (Aitken et al., 2021; Parker, 2018).

What is new is how these alternative ownership models *by design* are taking values-based approaches to mutualistic forms of ownership and corporate governance which are infused with a social mission and a purpose beyond maximising profits in the short-term. These mutualistic newer forms of organisation often as co-operatives, employee-owned enterprises and social enterprises is that they agree to share power and profits and have shared, generative prosperity as their goal *by design* which align with their founders' personal values. In the words of a new such financial co-operative, Zebra Unite, founded by four women to fund mutualistic start-ups, "These alternative models will balance profit and purpose, champion democracy, and put a premium on sharing power and resources. Companies that create a more just and responsible society will hear, help, and heal the customers and communities they serve" (Scholtz, 2020, p. 4). How economically viable these models are is yet to be established. Any gardener who knows anything good will be attacked, and generative model businesses may well fall prey to extractive businesses' strategic reactions to them. Marjorie Kelly's (2012) work concerning the values-guided generative business models distinguishes them from extractive forms of value creation as outlined below in Table 5.2.

There is bound to be exciting innovations in this values-guided generative space, as the wisdom of bio-mimicry and indigenous populations continues to diffuse. The business landscape is teeming with examples with social and ecological generative organisations which are concealed by the discourse of shareholder capitalism model as the only game in town projected by everyday business media and apostles of the Friedman doctrine published over 50 years ago that declared: "there is one and only one social purpose of business… to increase its profits so long as it stays within the rules of the game" (Friedman, 1970, p. 7).

Table 5.2 Extractive vs Generative forms of ownership architecture

Extractive ownership	*Generative ownership*
Absentee membership: majority ownership by disconnected shareholders	Rooted membership: ownership in humans connected to the life of the enterprise
Governance by Markets: Control by capital markets on autopilot	Mission-controlled governance: control by those dedicated to social mission
Financial purpose: maximising profits in the short-term	Living purpose: creating the conditions for life over the long-term
Casino finance: capital as master	Stakeholder finance: capital as friend
Commodity networks: trading focused on price & profit	Ethical networks: collective support for ecological and social norms

Source Adapted from Kelly (2012)

Meanwhile, the incrementalistic and Reformist adaptive strategies appealing to a majority of people's values will persist, outlined below.

5.3.2 Enterpriser and Settler Type Strategies: Incrementalism and Reform

Incrementalism and reforming the system are the other adaptive strategy-types, a type of template change with the purpose of improving the status quo. The proposition is that these types of strategies will be pursued by Enterprisers and only belatedly by Settlers out of survival. Incrementalistic approaches include Corporate Social Responsibility (CSR) initiatives and equity stake schemes such as employee share options (ESO) and profit-sharing schemes. It's sticking to the knitting whilst trying to improve a stitch.

Reformist agendas include 'ESG' companies who in theory adopt criteria including environmentally-friendly, social and/or governance policies. In practice, the devil is in the detail: companies with dubious credentials such as the digital dictators of Facebook, Apple, Amazon, Microsoft and Google are included in ESG portfolios. The work of Gregory et al. (2014) found that companies with a strong Environmental, Social and Governance (ESGs) profile are more competitive than their peers due to their more efficient use of resources, better human capital development, and/or better innovation management. A study by the investment research firm Morgan Stanley Capital International (MSCI) compared four global MSCI ESG indexes to their parent indexes during COVID-19 and found the ECGs outperformed the rest: they are less exposed to systematic risks including the coronavirus crisis (MSCI, 2020). As a 'doing things better' approach, this will appeal to Enterprises. The Big Four audit firms' $12bn investment in targeting 'ESG advice' over the next 5 years underscores the allure of fast followers to this approach, especially as they smell the profit earning potential in ESG advice (Edgecliffe-Johnson & O'Dwyer, 2021). PWC alone plans to hire 100,00 employees over the five years in ESG advice which has seen annual revenues grow by 20% and a workforce grow by more than a quarter to 284,00 for the same period (Edgecliffe-Johnson & O'Dwyer, 2021).

One of the main contributions of the reformist agenda has been Benefit Corporations or 'B corps', a relatively new type of legal entity created through a private certification process that requires companies to declare a social purpose in their governing documentation to meet independent standards of social, environmental, accountability and transparency performance. Although it has its critics as it is not a complete design, it is no doubt a positive step forward in the reformist agenda (Kelly, 2012).

To recap, the World Economic Forum's (2020) Global Risks Report declared that the renewing and improving the architecture of our economic systems and 'reimagining' business and it's adaptive strategies to social and economic challenges it faces 'is this generations defining task' (Brandel et al., 2020). Underscoring this debate are values-guided transformational strategies with the really exciting prospect of ownership, governance, finance and network architecture that align and in harmony with leaderships' leading edge personal values.

Within organisations, regardless of adaptive strategies adopted, values-guided deep dialogue about adaptive strategies must value values diversity such that all values-guided voices need to be heard. Explorers need Enterprisers to get their heads out of the clouds and focus on the bottom-line every bit as much as both Enterprisers and Explorers both need Settlers to keep their feet on the ground and ensure systems, structures and fiduciary responsibilities are adhered to.

The final section concludes with an emerging complementary lens to personal values, which addresses some of the shortcomings of the Upper Echelon Theory. In Chapter one the shortcomings of the Upper Echelon theory were discussed, namely that whether the personal values which guide senior management has to be ethical or not isn't addressed. Moreover, the dynamic of multiple stakeholders' values orientations is not included in the model (Freeman et al., 1988). The final section concerning moral tendencies and how it relates to internal and external stakeholders seeks to overcome these limitations.

5.4 Emerging Trends: Moral Tendencies and Personal Values Orientation

We return to the 'inner compass' guiding strategic decisions and actions discussed in chapter one that is related to personal values-guided strategy, which is the proposed relationship between moral tendencies, personal values and their impact on strategy and governance. Moral tendencies and personal values are different lenses, but future work may well explore how moral and ethical orientations vary by personal values.

It was the moral philosopher Adam Smith writing in his first book in 1795, *The Theory of Moral Sentiments*, who first observed consciousness and morality are the foundations of a well-functioning and prosperous society. Smith argued that responsibility and concepts like Corporate Social Responsibility (CSR) can only become reality if formal and informal leaders' practice being moral (Aitken et al., 2021). It was this that laid the foundation for the market system and his next book, The Wealth of Nations. Smith's inconvenient truth that morality and consciousness are the bedrock of a well-functioning market and society explains why free-market fundamentalists a 'senior moment' about his first book have but choose to amplify his second one.

Lichtenstein and Aitken's (2014) initially proposed that the natural world offers insights into moral tendencies and propose their relationship to personal values as summarised in Table 5.3.

In ecology, *symbiosis* is the study of biological interactions between organisms, however we extend this to those within the enterprise, and/or the relationship between the organisation and its external stakeholders and environment. Referring to the table above, *Mutualism* is any relationship between individuals of different species, where all parties benefit—a 'win–win' relationship. This has a notably moral orientation with benevolent intentions. *Commensalism* describes a relationship between two living organisms where one benefits and the other is not significantly harmed or helped. The word derives from Latin, formed from com and mensa, meaning 'sharing a table'. This represents an amoral inclination. By contrast, *Parasitism* based relationships are ones where only one member of the association benefits whilst the other is intentionally harmed, which has malevolent intentions done at the expense of others—'heads I win, tails you lose' relationship which is immoral.

When it comes to values-guided strategy, there is a moral dynamic at play, with people influenced by the prevailing mutual, commensalistic or

Table 5.3 Proposed links to symbiosis and morality tendencies

Symbiotic tendency	*Morality tendency*	*Kohlberg's (1976) Moral development phase*
Mutualism	Moral	Post conventional
Commensalism	Amoral	Conventional
Parasitism	Immoral	Pre-conventional

Source Adapted from Lichtenstein and Aitken (2014)

Table 5.4 Doing the right thing by values orientation

Settler	Enterprisers	Explorers
Rules/Authority: Follow the rules; do what the authority says	Success: Cost/benefit analysis of winning; visible success and ability that justifies the means	Ideals: Ethics—being true to oneself

Source Adapted by Lichtenstein et al. (2011) and Rose (2011)

parasitic intentions and relationships that confront us on a daily basis. Being aware of this interplay is a necessary first step in seeing and potentially making choices between short-term transactional relationships or longer term, more sustainable and mutually transformative ones (Aitken et al., 2021).

Below are propositions based on how doing the right thing may vary based on the different worldviews of Settlers, Enterprisers and Explorers. These are summarised in Table 5.4.

How moral leadership varies by values orientations' relates to the pioneering work of psychologist Kohlberg's (1976) work on moral development. We use Kohlberg's (1976) work to illustrate the 'typical' perspective of each values orientation for reflection, not as a prediction tool.

The *Settler* perspective most closely relates to Kohlberg's (1976) conventional phase whereby morality is about conforming to and upholding the rules and expectations of society or authority just because they are society's rules, expectations or conventions. The self has internalised the rules and expectations of others. Morality and conscience are defined by group rules, e.g. a religious group. This phase has two further substages: Stage A—the need to be seen as a good person in one's own eyes and those of others; Stage B—to keep society going as a whole, 'if everyone did 'x', society would be in chaos'.

Individuals who solely considers his or her interests and those of isolated individuals (friends, siblings, parents), and calculates the good or bad personal consequences which may arise are considered in the non-conventional phase of moral development in Kohlberg's (1976) levels: rules and expectations are external to the self and imposed. Stages at this level include Stage A—avoidance of punishment and Stage B—individualism to serve one's own needs. This may be best exemplified by the genuine puzzlement of Anglo-American financial traders and bankers at the criticism they received during the Great Financial Crash of 2008 (Rose, 2011). After all, they were only 'creating more wealth'—maximising results, hitting targets and getting bigger bonuses. They were only doing what the system asked them to do, what was wrong?

We propose that explorers relate closest to Kohlberg's (1976) Post-conventional Moral Phase who make personal decisions and decide internally; formulating and accepting ethical principles that underline the rules. When principles come into conflict with society's rules, post-conventional individuals judge by principle rather than convention. A post-conventional person differentiates his or herself from the rules and expectations of others and defines his or her values in terms of self-chosen principles: justice or fairness, and oriented towards liberty, equality, reciprocity and mutual rewarding relationships between persons. It can also encompass the 'ideal' self-orientation to an image of an actor as a good self, or as someone with a conscience, and to the self's motives or virtue. This phase has two stages A—abide by the law for the welfare and protection of all people's rights, and Stage B—self chosen ethical and universal principles of justice: the equality of human rights and respect for the dignity of human beings as individual persons.

It remains unclear to what extent people can move between these stages, when, and to what extent, moral preferences are defined earlier in life (before puberty), how relatively fixed they remain, and their proposed links to values orientations, all areas for further study.

Carroll's (1991) work below on moral governance orientations based on moral, amoral and immoral orientations and types of intent and mode of interaction with Owner-Shareholder, Employee, Customer and Local Community stakeholders makes these moral considerations relevant to organisation's relationship to its wider ecosystem.

Orientation Towards Owner/Shareholder Stakeholders
IMMORAL: Shareholders are minimally treated and given short shrift. Focus is on maximising positions of executive groups—maximising executive compensation, perks, benefits. Golden parachutes are more important than returns to shareholders. Managers maximise their positions without shareholders being made aware. Concealment from shareholders is the operating procedure. Self-interest of the management group is the order of the day.
AMORAL: No special thought is given to shareholders; they are there and must be minimally accommodated. Profit focus of the business is

their reward. No thought is given to ethical consequences of decisions for any stakeholder group, including owners. Communication is limited to that required by law.
MORAL: Shareholders' interest (short- and long-term) is a central factor. The best way to be ethical to shareholders is to treat all stakeholder claimants in a fair and ethical manner. To protect shareholders, an ethics committee of the board is created. Code of ethics is established, promulgated, and made a living document to protect shareholders' and others' interests.

Orientation Towards Employee Stakeholders
IMMORAL: Employees are viewed as factors of production to be used, exploited, manipulated for the gain of individual manager or company. No concern is shown for employees' needs/rights/expectations. Coercive, controlling and alienating behaviour dominates.
AMORAL: Employees are treated as the law requires. Attempts to motivate focus on increasing productivity rather than satisfying employees' growing maturity needs. Employees are still seen as factors of production with only a remunerative approach used. Organisation sees self-interest in treating employees with minimal respect. Organisation structure, pay incentives, rewards are all geared towards short- and medium-term productivity.
MORAL: Employees are a human resource that must be treated with dignity and respect. Goal is to use a leadership style such as consultative/participative that will result in mutual confidence and trust. Commitment is a recurring theme. Employees' rights to due process, privacy, freedom of speech, and safety are maximally considered in all decisions. Management seeks out fair dealings with employees.

Orientation Towards Customer Stakeholders
IMMORAL: Customers are viewed as opportunities to be exploited for personal or organisational gain. Ethical standards in dealings do not prevail; indeed, an active intent to cheat, deceive and/or mislead is present. In all marketing decisions—advertising, pricing, packaging, distribution, the customer is taken advantage of to the fullest extent.
AMORAL: Management does not think through the ethical consequences of its decisions and actions. It simply makes decisions with profitability within the letter of the law as a guide. Management is not focused on what is fair from the perspective of customers. Focus is on

management's rights. No consideration is given to ethical implications of interactions with customers.
MORAL: Customer is viewed as an equal partner in transactions. Customer brings needs/expectations to the exchange transaction and is treated fairly. Managerial focus is on giving customer fair value, full information, fair guarantee, and satisfaction. Consumer rights are liberally interpreted and honoured.

Orientation Towards Local Community Stakeholders
IMMORAL: Exploits community to the fullest extent. Actively disregards community needs. Takes fullest advantage of community resources without giving anything in return or considering the impact of livelihoods and lives.
AMORAL: Does not take community or its resources into account in management decision making. Community factors are assumed to be irrelevant to business decisions. Community, like employees, is a factor of production. Legal considerations are followed, but nothing more. Deals minimally with community, its people, community activity and local government.
MORAL: Sees community vitality as a goal to be actively pursued. Seeks to be a leading citizen and to motivate others to do likewise. Gets actively involved and helps institutions that need help—schools, recreational groups, philanthropic groups. Adopts a leadership position in environmental, education, culture/arts, volunteerism and general community affairs. Engages in strategic philanthropy. Management sees community goals and company goals as mutually interdependent.

The final section illustrates the Adam Smith-inspired concepts discussed in this section.

5.5 Personal Values-Guided Strategy: Sustainable Living Plan

Unilever was under ex-CEO Paul Polman's stewardship for 10 years (who is now chair of global business collective Imagine). The company implemented its ambitious Sustainable Living Plan and set the goals to double its growth, halve its environmental impact and triple its social impact (Aziz, 2020). The plan succeeded, with Unilever's annual sales rising from $38 billion to more than $60 billion. As a publicly-traded company with shareholders, on his first day as a CEO he announced he would no longer be issuing quarterly share guidance and reports to break free of the tyranny of short-termism. The long-term approach with stretch goals paid off: Unilever delivered a total shareholder return of 290% over his tenure.

Importantly, the Sustainable Living Plan and aligned stretched goals was the product of 'a crucible moment' in Polman's life. He was in the Taj Mahal Hotel in Mumbai in 2008 when terrorists attacked the hotel and he and his team were trapped there for hours until they were rescued by the police in the early hours of the morning. In total, 172 people died in attacks across the city. The experience made Polman realise the profound link between poverty and violence. "What you then realize is that a lot of the violence in the world is driven by poverty and by exclusion, which religious fanatics seize upon and create these extreme forms of violence, which we should never give into. And that helped me when we did the Unilever Sustainable Living plan. So many companies with purpose are on the side of the environment which was very narrowly defined as trees and water and conservation. But it runs much deeper. We need to fight for addressing these issues of exclusion and poverty, which are at the roots of this violence. And so if you don't understand that human dimension, and that the crisis we face is one of humanity more so than anything else, you can't really properly solve it" (Aziz, 2020, p. 1).

What Polman's example reminds us of is that values-guided strategy comes from the hearts and minds of people; healthy strategies require healthy minds. Beyond the mind is consciousness, and the farther reaches of personal values-guided strategy will explore this relationship. Strategies from a conscious awareness that we are one humanity on this planet which we share with other sentient beings as part of the universe is radically different than strategies grounded in a mechanical intelligence based on conquest. Fulfillment, not mere achievement, can be realised when the goal becomes conscious strategic choice-making that nourishes our values as well as everyone else influenced by our actions. When we as strategists embed our thinking in stewardship such as Polman—responsibly caring for something we value as a path to realising our and our organisation's dreams—there is a qualitative difference in ends: taking care of our children's well-being, making healthy choices for our customer's bodies or using earth's natural resources responsibly versus being solely fixated on increasing market share, sales revenue or boosting operating profit margin by another 2%.

We trust it will not take another tragic accident for future informal and formal business leaders to pursue similar moral and values-guided strategies embedded in consciousness. May we all contribute to value creating strategies in Adman Smith's words that create a well-functioning and prosperous society that delivers 'happiness of a great community' to experience abundance, growth and fulfilment.

5.6 Summary

In this chapter, personal values guided strategy was put in a historical context of the management issue lifecycle. The emerging trend of values-guided transformational strategy and generative ownership architecture in the context of the adaptive strategies of reformist and incremental was linked to the values orientations of Explorers, Enterprisers and Settlers, respectively. To enhance understanding of the invisible forces having a visible impact on strategic decisions and choices affecting a variety of stakeholders, emerging links between moral orientations with personal values was made. Paul Polman's morally and values-guided Sustainable Living Plan illustrates how personal values-guided strategy based on stewardship principles that value people and planet brings prosperity and riches in all its guises far beyond mere profitability.

Bibliography

Aitken, P., Villoslada, P. Lichtenstein, S., & de Lecea, L. (2021). *Adam Smith Revisited: Moral Leadership for Global Recovery and Restoration.* In Review.

Andrews, K. R. (1980). *The concept of corporate strategy* (Rev.). R.D. Irwin Inc.

Aziz, A. (2020, May 25). *Paul Polman on courageous CEOs and how purpose is the growth story of the century (Part 1).* Forbes. https://www.forbes.com/sites/afdhelaziz/2020/05/25/paul-polman-on-purpose-courageous-ceos-and-the-growth-story-of-the-century-part-1/?sh=5df8834a1dfd. Accessed 4 December 2020.

Barnosky, A. D., et al. (2012). Approaching a state shift in Earth's biosphere. *Nature, 486*, 52–58.

Barrett, R. (1998). *Liberating the corporate soul.* Routledge.

Brandel, J., Zepeda, M., Scholtz, A., & Williams, A. (2020, July 30). *Pivot to people: It's time to build the new economy.* https://medium.com/zebras-unite/pivot-to-people-its-time-to-build-the-new-economy-75a624eaf38a. Accessed 16 March 2021.

Carrington, D. (2019, October 13). Firms ignoring climate crisis will go bankrupt, says Mark Carney. *Guardian*.

Carroll, A. B. (1991, July-August). The pyramid of corporate social responsibility: Toward the moral management of organizational stakeholders. *Business Horizons, 34*, 39–48.

Ecological Footprint. (2021). https://www.footprintnetwork.org/our-work/ecological-footprint/. Accessed 13 July 2021.

Edgecliffe-Johnson, E., & O'Dwyer, M. (2021, June 15). *PwC to boost headcount by 100,000 over five years*. The FT. https://www.ft.com/content/b79e4cd4-e288-4083-a976-47f3e89a0209. Accessed 5 August 2021.

Finkelstein, S., & Hambrick, D. (1998). *Strategic leadership; Top executives and their effects on organisations*. West Educational Publishing.

Freeman, R. E., Gilbert, D. R., & Hartman, E. (1988). Values and the foundations of strategic management. *Journal of Business Ethics, 7*(11), 821–834.

Friedman, M. (1970, September 13). A Friedman doctrine—The social responsibility of business is to increase its profits. *New York Times*.

Gregory, A., Tharyan, R., & Whittaker, J. (2014). Corporate social responsibility and firm value: Disaggregating the effects on cash flow, risk and growth. *Journal of Business Ethics, 124*(4), 633–657.

Guth, W. D., & Tagiuri, R. (1965). Personal values and corporate-strategy. *Harvard Business Review, 43*(5), 123–132.

Hambrick, D. C., & Mason, P. A. (1984). Upper echelons: The organization as a reflection of its top managers. *Academy of Management Review, 9*(2), 193–206.

IPPC. (2021). *Report*. https://www.ipcc.ch/report/sixth-assessment-report-cycle/. Accessed 13 August 2021.

Kelley, E. L. (1927). *Interpretation of educational measurements*. World Book.

Kelly, M. (2012). *Owning our future: The emerging ownership revolution*. Berrett-Koehler Publishers.

Kohlberg, L. (1976). Moral stages and moralization: The cognitive-developmental approach. In T. Lickona (Ed.), *Moral development and behavior: Theory, research, and social issues* (pp. 31–53). Holt, Rinehart & Winston.

Lichtenstein, S., & Aitken, P. (2014). *The values challenge for developing ethical leadership: Research and practice agenda for values-based leadership*. 6th Developing Leadership Capacity Conference, Lancaster University.

Lichtenstein, S., & Dade, P. (2007). The shareholder value chain: Values, vision and shareholder value creation. *Journal of General Management, 33*(1), 15–31.

Lichtenstein, S., Higgins, L., & Dade, P. (2011). Integrity in the boardroom: A case for further research. In *Corporate governance and business ethics* (pp. 307–326). Springer, Dordrecht.

Mackie, D., & Murray, J. (2020, January 14). Risky business: The climate and the macroeconomy. *Economic Research*. J. P. Morgan Securities.

Mintzberg, H., Ahlstrad, B., & Lampel, J. (1998). *Strategy Safari: A guide through the wilds of strategic management*. Free Press.

Mintzberg, H., Lampel, J., Quinn, J., & Ghoshal, S. (2003). *Strategy process: Concepts, contexts, cases*. Pearson Education.

MSCI. (2020, April 22). *ESG Indexes during the coronavirus crisis*: https://www.msci.com/www/blog-posts/msci-esg-indexes-during-the/01781235361. Accessed 26 April 2020.

Parker, M. (2018). *Shut down the business school: What's wrong with management education*. Pluto Press.

Peters, T., & Waterman, R. (1982). *In search of excellence*. Harper & Row.

Powell, T. C., Lovallo, D., & Fox, C. R. (2011). Behavioral strategy. *Strategic Management Journal, 32*(13), 1369–1386.

Raworth, K. (2021). *Foundations of doughnut economics*. Ubiquity University.

Rose, C. (2011). *What Makes People Tick: The three hidden worlds of settlers, prospectors and pioneers*. Matador.

Rushe, D. (2021). Green investing 'is definitely not going to work', says ex-BlackRock executive. *The Guardian*, Tuesday, March 30. https://www.theguardian.com/business/2021/mar/30/tariq-fancy-environmentally-friendly-green-investing?CMP=Share_iOSApp_Other. Accessed 30 March 2021

Scholz, A. (2020, February 2). *Where unicorns fear to tread—Building businesses that are better for the world*. A short history of Zebras Unite. https://medium.com/zebras-unite/where-unicorns-fear-to-tread-building-businesses-that-are-better-for-the-world-35190e632c9e. Accessed 16 March 2021.

Smith, A. (1976). *The theory of moral sentiments* (D. D. Raphael & A. L. Macfie, Eds.). Clarendon Press.

Smith, A. (2016). *The wealth of nations*. Aegitas.

Ubiquity University. (2021). https://www.ubiquityuniversity.org/courses/mra-masters-in-regenerative-action/. Accessed 7 August 2021.

United Nations. (2015). *Sustainable development goals*. https://sdgs.un.org/goals.

World Economic Forum. (2020, January 15). *The Global Risks Report*. https://www.weforum.org/reports/the-global-risks-report-2020

WWF. (2020). *Living planet report*. https://livingplanet.panda.org/en-us/. Accessed 7 August 2020.

Annex: UN Sustainability Development Goals

Source UN

S. Lichtenstein and M. Higgs, *Strategy through Personal Values*,
https://doi.org/10.1007/978-3-030-88269-3

Index

S. Lichtenstein and M. Higgs, *Strategy through Personal Values*,
https://doi.org/10.1007/978-3-030-88269-3

The manufacturer's authorised representative in the EU is Springer Nature Customer Service Centre GmbH, Europaplatz 3, 69115 Heidelberg, Germany. If you have any concerns regarding our products, please contact ProductSafety@springernature.com

Printed and bound by CPI Group (UK) Ltd, Croydon, CR0 4YY
30/09/2026
02225472-0004